KENDO
The Definitive Guide

KENDO
The Definitive Guide

HIROSHI OZAWA

Translated by Angela Turzynski
Illustrated by Tamiko Yamaguchi

KODANSHA INTERNATIONAL
Tokyo • New York • London

The official regulations that appear in the appendices are reproduced with the permission of the International Kendo Federation.

The list of Kendo clubs around the world could not have been compiled without the cooperation of the relevant national federations and associations.

Photo credits: Kendo Nippon, pp. 1, 51, 57, 121, 135; Itsukushima Shrine, p. xi.

This book was originally published in Japanese by Baseball Magazine Sha in 1991.

Distributed in the United States by Kodansha America, Inc., 575 Lexington Avenue, New York, New York 10022, and in the United Kingdom and continental Europe by Kodansha Europe Ltd., 95 Aldwych, London WC2B 4JF. Published by Kodansha International Ltd., 17-14 Otowa 1-chome, Bunkyo-ku, Tokyo 112-8652, and Kodansha America, Inc. Copyright © 1997 by Hiroshi Ozawa. English translation © 1997 by Kodansha International Ltd. All rights reserved. Printed in Japan.

ISBN 4-7700-2119-4

First edition, 1997

03 04 05   10 9 8 7

CIP data available

www.thejapanpage.com

CONTENTS

PREFACE

I have been overseas perhaps a dozen times, and each time I have made a point of visiting libraries and bookstores in whatever town or city I happened to be in. Not once, however, have I come across a book on Kendo, despite the fact that thirty-six Kendo groups from thirty-four countries are currently affiliated with the International Kendo Federation. The World Kendo Championship Title Tournament, held once every three years, bears witness to the increasing international interest in this traditional Japanese sport.

I hope that this book will not only serve as a guide to those people already engaged in Kendo, but that it will also inspire those who are at present unfamiliar with the sport to take it up. For, if practiced correctly, I believe that there is no martial art as safe and as effective both for the mind and the body as Kendo. I hope, therefore, that schools and public libraries will add this book to their collections.

Finally, I should like to express my sincere appreciation to Angela Turzynski, who translated this book, to Julian McManus for his helpful advice, and to Paul Hulbert of Kodansha International.

Hiroshi Ozawa

INTRODUCTION

1. What Is Kendo?

The practice of Kendo as a physical activity has a long tradition within Japanese culture. Originally a method of sword manipulation, Kendo came to be more fully understood through observance of natural laws on the battlefield. It can be divided into the following three components:

(1) The way of the body—how to hold the sword, *maai* (spatial distance separating two opponents), etc.

(2) The way of the sword—how to execute a strike, the right moment to execute a strike, etc.

(3) The way of the mind—the correct mental attitude.

While these divisions represent a useful basis for a theoretical understanding of the main elements of Kendo, in practice they are closely interlinked, with the distinction between them not always so clear. Nevertheless, it is essential that those learning Kendo first acquire a grasp of these basic components and realize that the practice of Kendo is more than a simple matter of overcoming an opponent.

2. Why Practice Kendo?

Kendo has been practiced for various purposes at different stages of its development, according to the prevailing social conditions of the era. While everyone beginning Kendo will have their own particular motive, the aim of Kendo today may be said to be the development of a healthy body and mind through a sustained period of practice (*keiko*). In Japan, between four and five million people practice Kendo in schools, workplaces, and police stations, as well as in *dōjō*s.

Present-day Kendo is a technique which enables a strike to be executed on an opponent in a previously determined spot, by means of a *shinai* (bamboo sword). In this sense, Kendo may be likened to a modern sport. However, we should also retain the spirit of Kendo, which has survived through the ages as an unbroken tradition. The original motto of Kendo was "Victory means survival, defeat means death." Although today this is not to be taken literally, it is important to adopt a serious attitude toward the practice of Kendo, with the aim of forming a rounded human being, incorporating physical, spiritual, and social development.

Below are some hints which may be helpful for the understanding of Kendo practice:

(1) In the *dōjō*, dispense with any easy sense of camaraderie. As long as you

are wearing the *men* (mask), the opponent must be perceived as the enemy, and *keiko* (practice) carried out as a one-on-one confrontation.

(2) It should be recognized that each person has his or her own style and philosophy of Kendo which should be respected while still maintaining a sense of harmony in the group.

(3) *Keiko* should be carried out with the whole self—spirit (*kihaku*), physical strength, and technique.

(4) Each *keiko*, and each strike delivered during *keiko*, should be performed as if it were the one and only chance you have.

(5) Through *keiko*, strive hard to develop the self.

(6) Improve your Kendo by devoting yourself to *keiko* for its own sake.

It should always be remembered that Kendo is not something you know, but rather something you enjoy learning. Kendo is therefore something you become good at unconciously, over a period of time.

3. Adopt a Generous and Liberal Attitude toward Your Opponent

Despite passing through various stages of development, the essence (*honshitsu*) of Kendo has remained constant: one person faces another, ready with the *shinai*, mind meets mind, and the opponents strike. By training one's spirit and performing *keiko* correctly, honestly, and full of vigor, an ennobling of human nature takes place.

This may initially appear paradoxical, for how can human nature be ennobled by the act of looking for an opponent's unguarded moment and executing a strike?

To appreciate this it should be realized that Kendo today is practiced in an environment removed from the everyday world. The act of attacking and parrying is carried out with the implicit understanding that no one actually intends to kill or wound an opponent. Rather, in engaging in such an act, opponents both compete and cooperate with one another. Always remember to respect your opponent and to recognize his or her human nature, while at the same time resisting with all your might. In this way, each can ennoble the human nature of the other. Competition rules exist precisely to help maintain this vital balance.

In addition, while winning a match is important in Kendo, it is equally important to conquer yourself in the difficult situation in which you are placed. In other words, it is essential when learning Kendo to form a spirit of self-denial, which will lead to an ennobling of the self.

4. Women and Kendo

The number of women taking up Kendo in the U.S. today exceeds the figure for men. Furthermore, it is predicted that this trend will continue into the next century, so that eventually more women than men will be practicing Kendo. Although the reasons for this are unclear, it would seem that Kendo offers women something that other martial arts do not.

Large numbers of women have long been attracted to such martial arts as Judo and Aikido, often out of a desire to equip themselves with some form of self-defense skills. Kendo, however, requiring the use of specialized armor, does not fit into this category of martial art. It must be assumed, therefore, that women are taking it up for other reasons, some of them no doubt similar to those cited by women in Japan who practice Kendo. Not only does Kendo help to relieve stress and bring about a feeling of physical and mental well-being—many other sports may do this just as well—but it also teaches assertiveness. Moreover, this can be cultivated in a non-threatening environment since, unlike the case of most other martial arts, the use of armor in Kendo means that no actual body contact takes place.

It should be stressed that the Kendo practiced by women is exactly the same in every way as that practiced by men. Since the basis of Kendo is not physical strength but correct *waza* and proper mental attitude, it is equally suitable for both men and women, and the current trend in the U.S. is therefore extremely encouraging.

THE HISTORY OF KENDO

The Era of the Genji and Heike Clans—The Origins of the Kendo Ethos

From the early tenth century, armed bands of horsemen known as *tsuwamono*, *mono-no-fu*, or *samurai* arose in the Kantō region (around Tokyo), far from the political center of Kyoto. Initially, these rough, unsophisticated bands were comprised of members of the chieftain's own family, so that warriors and farmers formed a single, unified group. By the twelfth century, however, outsiders had come to be included, creating a stratified lord and vassal system in which the retainers were known as *ie-no-ko* or *rōdō*. The Genji and Heike clans were two such armed bands. The illustration shows *ōyoroi*, magnificent ceremonial armor worn by military commanders on the battlefield, as depicted in the thirteenth-century literary classic, *Heike Monogatari* (*The Tale of the Heike*), a military epic which vividly records the rise and fall of the Heike or Taira clan.

Bushidō, or "The Way of the Samurai," the feudal-military Japanese code of behavior, has its roots in this era. Though initially specialists in armed combat, the *mono-no-fu* developed quite early on an unwritten moral code, which placed great emphasis on the virtues of loyalty, valor, honor, and shame. The *mono-no-fu* on the battlefield was unstintingly brave, drawing a strong bow from astride his horse, and always ready to face the enemy head-on. He abhorred cowardly acts, such as turning one's back to flee the enemy, or felling a horse in order to kill the rider. The *mono-no-fu* showed respect and consideration toward women. And he preferred to die rather than accept an insult.

Defeat of the Heike or Taira clan finally came in 1185, following which the chieftain of the victorious Genji or Minamoto clan established a new, exclusively military government known as the Shogunate. From this period onward, the power of the samurai rose to prominence, and what had begun with the combative skills of the *mono-no-fu* developed into something which went beyond a simple repertoire of martial techniques to incorporate a strict moral code of conduct and atti-

Twelfth century *ōyoroi*

tude of mind. The result was "the Way of the Samurai," and the medieval period was to provide ample opportunity for its further development and refinement. The Muromachi Shogunate in particular, from 1336–1573, was the most turbulent period in Japanese history, with wars raging almost constantly.

The Warring States Period (1467–1568)

The Ōnin War (1467–77), a dispute over the shogunal succession which resulted in the almost total devastation of the capital, Kyoto, was followed by a century of hostilities known as the "Warring States Period." The battles that raged during this period were mainly internecine struggles between vassal factions employing only weapons of a particular kind—lance, bow, musket, etc. However, though they were referred to as group battles, when it came to close combat, victory or defeat was determined by the fighting technique of the individual. To protect themselves from being overpowered by the enemy, therefore, the military commanders had to learn various martial arts.

During this era, three schools of fencing emerged.

1. *Tenshinshōdenshintōryū* School (founded by Iizasa Chōisai)
   Disciples included:
   Tsukamoto Bokuden

2. *Aisukageryū* School (founded by Aisu Ikōsai)
   Disciples included:
   Kamiizumi Ise-no-kami Hidetsuna
   Yagyū Sekishūsai
   Marume Kurando

3. *Ittōryū* School (founded by Chūjō Hyōgo-no-kami Nagahide)
   Disciples included:
   Itō Ittōsai

Although there were countless other master fencers, the founders of the above schools, Iizasa, Aisu, and Chūjō, are the most famous, and considered to be the oldest martial arts specialists. Other master fencers were employed by the *daimyō* (feudal lords), who not only received personal instruction from these veterans but also made sure that their retainers learned their secrets, too.

Edo Period (1603–1868)

After the divisive turbulence of the Muromachi period, Japan was finally unified under the Tokugawa Shogunate, eventually closing her doors to the West as a result of the perceived threat of Christianity and the potential danger of European armed support for the opponents of the new regime. Spanning more than 260 years, this was an age in which much of what is now considered traditionally Japanese in the realms of art and culture was nurtured and flourished. Kendo is one example.

The master fencers who were active in the Warring States period had possessed neither equipment nor armor, so that *keiko* consisted of wielding the *tachi* (long sword) and *bokutō* (wooden sword), learning *kata* from the master and striking a tree to polish technique. For *shiai* (matches), real swords or *bokutō* were used. The Edo period, however, saw the gradual appearance of *dōjō*s, and improvement in the design of *shinai* and armor. In the eighteenth century, *keiko* in the *dōjō*, protected by armor and exchanging blows with the *shinai*, became the norm. In fact, by the closing days of the Tokugawa regime as many as five or six hundred schools were said to have emerged.

However, this new method of practice came in for considerable criticism, being denounced as virtually useless in a real-life conflicts. When considered in the light of what had been proclaimed as the essence of fencing—fighting with swords on the battlefield where "victory is survival, defeat is death"—this was certainly a fair criticism. But this type of controlled and regulated practice nevertheless constituted an important stage in the development of Kendo.

Miyamoto Musashi and *Gorin-no-Sho* (*A Book of Five Rings*)

Not only in Japan but all over the world, one figure who stands out prominently among Japanese fencers is Miyamoto Musashi. This is largely due to Yoshikawa Eiji's novel *Musashi*, and Victor Harris's English translation of *Gorin-no-Sho* (*A Book of Five Rings*) which appeared in 1974. Not a great deal is known for certain about this master fencer, who lived during the turbulent decades between the age of provincial wars and the Edo period. However, *Gorin-no-Sho* includes some autobiographical detail, which I will present here.

Musashi was born in 1584, and learned martial arts from his father. His debut match at the age of thirteen gave him his first taste of victory, and from then on he never once suffered defeat in all the sixty or more matches he fought in his lifetime. After winning his most famous duel against Sasaki Kojirō in 1612, at the age of twenty-nine, Musashi immediately retired into seclusion, devoting himself to the search after the truth of the sword. It is said that he finally mastered the essence of the sword some twenty years later, at the age of around fifty.

Written when Musashi was sixty years old, *Gorin-no-Sho* embodies a comprehensive summary of his personal way of the sword, elaborated during his years of solitude. In it, he develops in detail his theory of strategy and his philosophy of life. In a nutshell, Musashi advocates the devotion of all one's energies to overcoming the enemy, including psychological strategy. The extremely practical form and logical style he employs to express his ideas is perhaps one reason why the English translation, *A Book of Five Rings*, has been so highly acclaimed in the West, not only for its value as an aid to understanding martial arts, but also for the techniques it contains both for successful business management and success in life.

Meiji Period to the Present (1868 onward)

In 1868, almost seven hundred years of continuous military rule came to an end, and the Emperor Meiji was restored to the throne. Within the ensuing climate of sweeping reform in an all-out attempt to modernize Japan in line with the newly industrialized Western powers, *kenjutsu* (the art of the sword) was seen as an undesirable relic of the samurai class, now officially dissolved in an attempt to establish legal equality for all. Thereafter, the art of the sword inevitably began to decline.

However, in 1887, twenty years into the Emperor Meiji's reign, the superficial Westernization which had been promoted so avidly began to be called into question, and a new policy of national wealth and military strength based on nationalism was initiated. In particular, the Japanese victory in the Sino-Japanese War (1894–1895) led to a heightened national awareness, and it was in this climate that Kendo began once again to attract attention as a method of juvenile education, with a movement rapidly developing for the incorporation of Kendo into the physical education curriculum as a core subject.

The Manchurian Incident of 1931 marked another important stage in Kendo's revival. Japan's seizure of Manchuria heralded a strengthening of the tendency toward militaristic nationalism, bolstered by the doctrine of the genius of the nation. Kendo now began to be valued very highly as one pillar of nationalist education.

In 1945, World War II ended with Japan's total surrender. Kendo's association with militaristic aggression, with all its devastating consequences, led to a ban being imposed by the American Occupation authorities on its practice, a ban which remained in force throughout the Occupation years. Then in October 1952 the All Japan Kendo Federation was formed on the principle of Kendo not as a martial art but as an educational sport, and it has continued to be practiced as such to this day.

Chapter

THE BASICS

Mokuso

Correct Fastening of *Keiko-gi* and *Hakama*

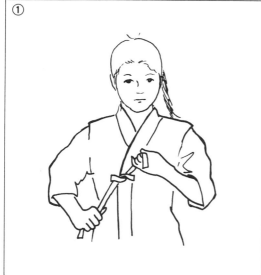

③ Pass the two *mae-himo* around the back, cross right over left, and bring round to the front. Bring the right *mae-himo* across the pelvis and twist the *mae-himo* (held by the right hand) upward, as in ④.

④ Cross over in front, and pass once again around the back.

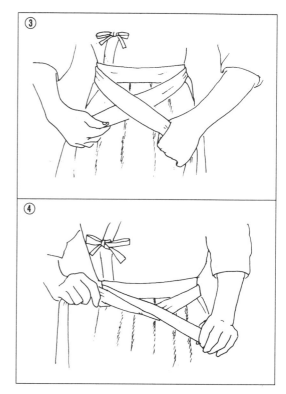

① Fasten the front of the *keiko-gi* (jacket) left over right, tying the *mune-himo* (chest string) in a bow.

② Step into the *hakama* (skirt), and place the *mae-himo* (belt) at waist level.

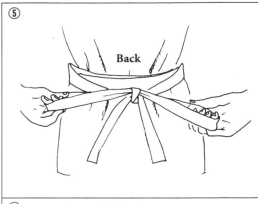

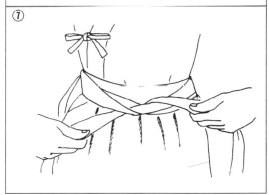

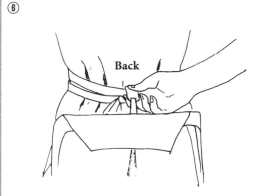

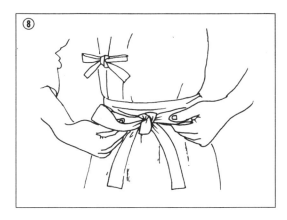

⑧ Tie in a bow at the center of the pelvic region. Finally, smooth out any creases in the *keiko-gi*.

⑤ Tie in a bow at the back.

⑥ Take hold of the *koshiita* (plastic spatula) and insert it from above into the *mae-himo*.

⑦ Bring the *ushiro-himo* around to the front and cross right over left in the center. Pass the left part of the *ushiro-himo* underneath and through the *mae-himo*, and pull firmly upward.

How to Put on *Kendōgu* (Armor)

(1) *Tare* (Waist Protector)

① Place the *tare-obi* in the center of the body at waist level.

② Pass the *koshi-himo* around the back, and cross the two sides below the *koshiita*. Pull firmly, taking care not to use too much force as this could lead to stomach pain during practice.

①

②

③

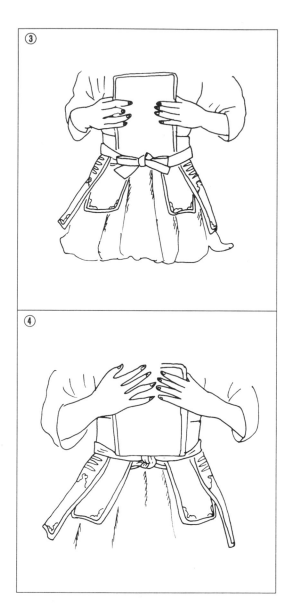

④

③ Bring the *koshi-himo* around to the front, and tie in a bow below the *ōdare*.

④ Insert the loose ends of the *koshi-himo* inside the left and right *kodare*.

(2) *Dō* (Body)

① Place the *dō* against the chest. Any necessary height adjustments can be made by moving the left *himo* toward the right shoulder or vice-versa.

② Pass the *himo* through the *chigawa* (loop) from back to front, as in fig. ②.

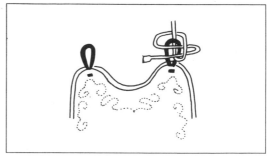

How to tie the *dō-himo*

①

②

③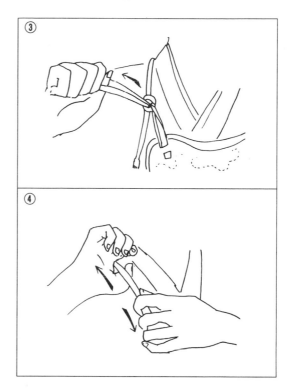

③ Pull the loop of the *dō-himo* and adjust the remaining *himo* to the same length, as shown in the illustration, "How to tie the *dō-himo*."

④ A tighter knot can be secured by holding the *dō-himo* just above the knot and pulling down with your left hand while pulling up with your right hand.

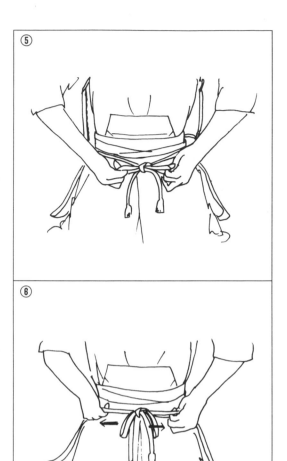

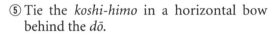

⑤ Tie the *koshi-himo* in a horizontal bow behind the *dō*.

⑥ Tighten the knot by pulling the *koshi-himo* firmly on each side.

⑦ Make sure the *dō* is straight.

The importance of using well-fitting *kendōgu* cannot be overemphasized. Young Kendoists, in particular, should take special care when purchasing this expensive piece of equipment. Sometimes it may be necessary to adjust the height of the *dō* so that all vulnerable areas are equally protected.

∗ The *mune-himo* can also be tied in a bow behind the neck. This method is suitable only for young children who are unable to tie it at the *chigawa*. They should, however, be taught the standard method as soon as they are judged capable.

(3) *Tenugui* (Traditional Hand Towel)
Method 1: Cap Style

① Spread the *tenugui* out flat.

② Fold in half, lengthwise.

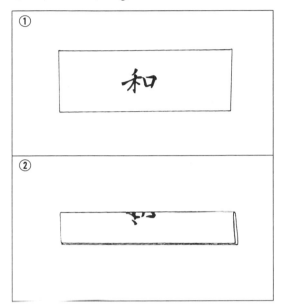

③④ Starting with either side, fold each side diagonally downward to fit the size of your head.

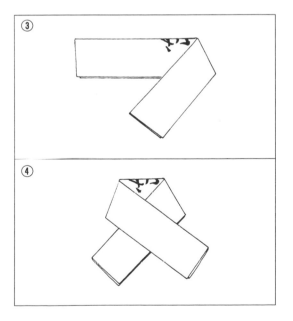

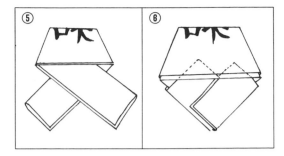

⑤ Turn the *tenugui* over.

⑥ Fold the protruding edges and tuck inside.

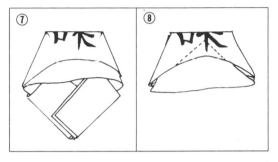

⑦⑧ Take the top point of the protruding triangle of cloth and fold upward, tucking it into the space between the two halves of the folded *tenugui*.

⑨ Place on your head with the thickest side at the front, making sure that the bangs are covered.

Method 2

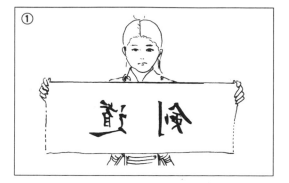

① Take hold of the *tenugui* from the top corners and hold it open.

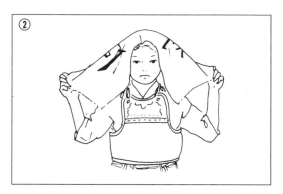

② Place the *tenugui* on your face and slide it back over your forehead, so that the edge held by your fingers comes down to cover the back of your head.

③ Fold each corner of the *tenugui* in turn across your forehead, so that they reach the opposite side, behind your ears.

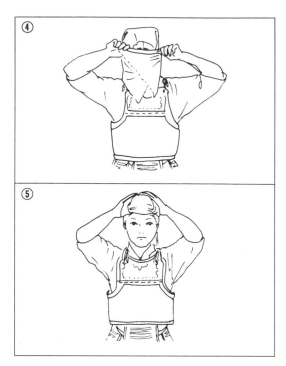

④⑤ Taking hold of the lower edge of the *tenugui* hanging down in front of your face, lift onto the top of your head and flatten it down firmly with both hands.

⑥ The *tenugui* should now:

- be wrapped fully around your hairline;
- not cover your ears;
- be securely in place so that it is not likely to come undone and slip down during *keiko*.

(4) *Men* (Head Gear)

① Holding the *men-himo* between the thumb and forefinger of each hand, push both sides of the *men-buton* (cloth part of *men*) outward.

② The *men* should fit snugly on your lower jaw and forehead.

③ Pull each *men-himo* firmly to the left and right.

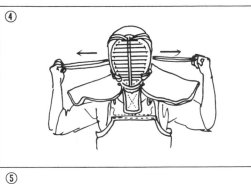

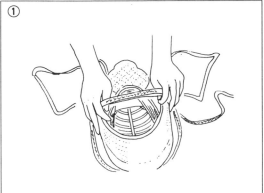

①

②

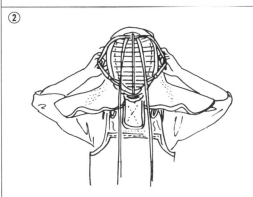

③

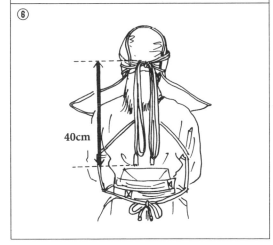

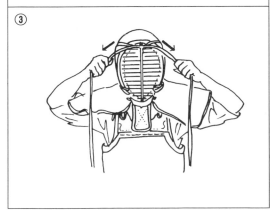

40cm

④ Tie in a bow behind your head. The bows should be of equal length to the strings.

⑤ Make sure the *men-himo* are not twisted, and then arrange them side by side.

⑥ To secure the bow, pull firmly on the strings behind to the left and right. The length of the *men-himo* should be no more than 40 cm from the knot. Take care to ensure that the *men-himo* are of equal length as shown in the illustration.

(5) *Kote* (Gloves)

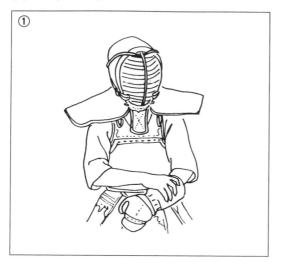

① Always put on the left *kote* first.

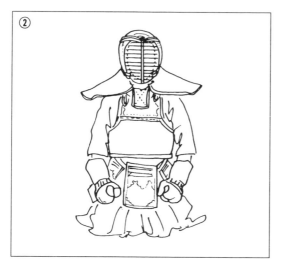

② The armor is now complete.

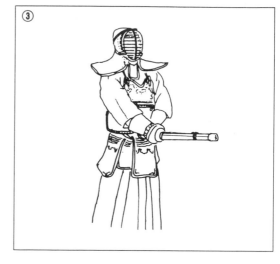

③ There will inevitably be a gap between the *dō-mune* and *tsuki-dare* (throat protector).

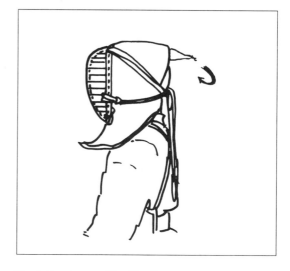

Tuck the *tenugui* inside the *men*.

It is not considered good form to begin *keiko* with part of the *tenugui* sticking out from the back of the *men*. Remember to tuck in the *tenugui* as soon as you put on your *men*. Alternatively, tidying up this loose end before donning your *men* is preferable. Never forget that in Kendo, the way you look from behind is just as important as the way you look from the front.

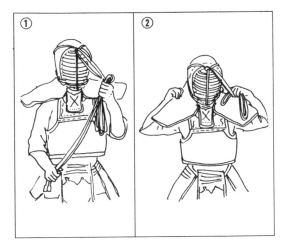

Place both *kote* down horizontally with the fists pointing out to one side of your right knee. Position the *shinai* to your left (ready for the next action).

After putting on your *men*, check that no further adjustments are necessary. Next, place your *kote* in a position that will enable you to put them on quickly. Careful preparation and attention to detail facilitates the next step: put on your *kote*, take hold of the *shinai* (bamboo sword), and stand.

Put on the *men* quickly and firmly.

Procrastination and idle chatter can waste valuable practice time and even disrupt *keiko*. Never fail to put on the *men* promptly and without fuss. Make sure that it is comfortable and tight enough not to come loose during *keiko*.

Before removing the *men*, arrange the *men-himo*.

① Overcome the temptation to remove your *men* immediately after *keiko* is over. Untie the *men-himo* carefully and patiently; take off your *men* only after arranging the *men-himo*.

② Holding the *men-himo*, take off your *men* and lay it on top of your *kote*, placing the *men-himo* inside. Sit in the *seiza* or "kneeling" position. Failure to remove the *men* patiently and competently as described above will mean that you will have to spend extra time untangling the *men-himo* at this stage.

Putting Away *Kendōgu*

① Wrap the *koshi-obi* (waist-belt) of the *tare* around the *tare-obi* and tuck the end of the *koshi-obi* inside.

②③ Place the *tare* on top of the *dō*.

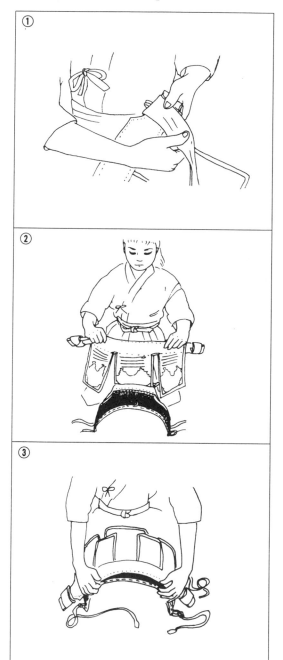

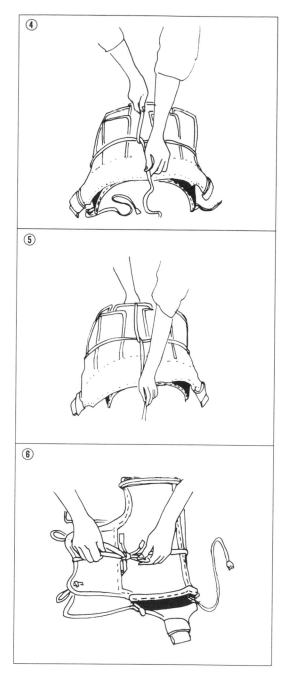

④ Cross over the left and right *mune-himo* of the *dō* in the middle.

⑤⑥ Pulling firmly on the *mune-himo*, take hold of the *dō* and turn it over. Next, tie the *mune-himo* in a bow on the inside of the *dō* at the center.

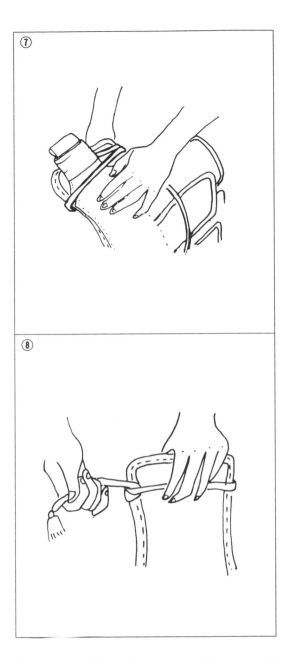

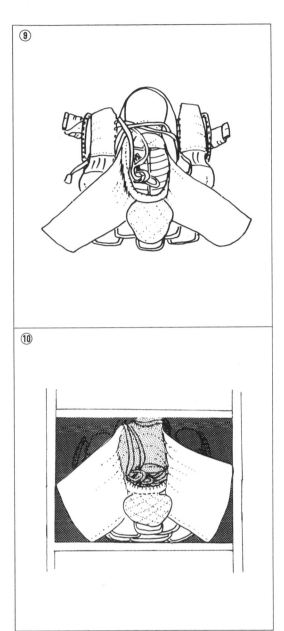

⑦ Wind the *koshi-himo* around the *tare-obi* so that it pushes against the *koshi-obi*, securing the *tare-obi* against the *dō*. Although the method itself is not so important, take care that both the left and right edges of the *tare-obi* are fixed.

⑧ Wind the *koshi-himo* around itself a few times so that it will not come loose.

⑨ When both sides have been secured, place the *kote* and the *men* inside the *dō*.

⑩ If the *kendōgu* is kept in a rack, it should be inserted with the front of the *men* first as shown in the illustration.

How to Fold *Keiko-gi* and *Hakama*

Proper care of *keiko-gi* and *hakama* is an essential part of Kendo. During *keiko*, these garments will absorb body perspiration and become soiled and smelly. Obviously, this is unhealthy for the wearer and offensive for others at the *dōjō*. Always remember to launder your *keiko-gi* and *hakama* after every *keiko* practice.

As we saw above with the *kendōgu*, there is a correct way to fold the *keiko-gi* and *hakama*.

Keiko-gi

① Open out the *keiko-gi* with the side seams aligned.

② Fold one side inward to about half the width of the *mae-migoro* (front part of the *keiko-gi*). Next fold over the sleeve.

③ Repeat the directions in ② for the opposite side.

④ Fold the bottom third upward.

⑤ Fold the top third downward, so that the *keiko-gi* is folded into three.

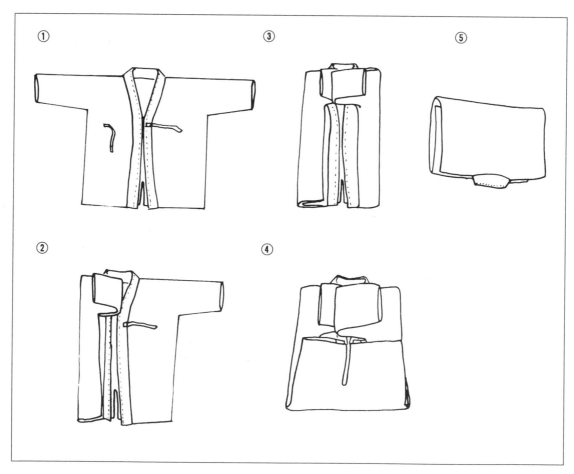

Hakama

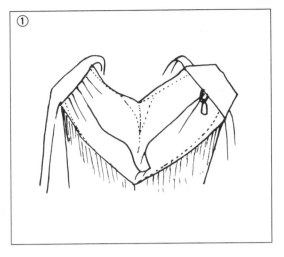

① Place your hand inside the *hakama* from the side and move the crotch seam to the right.

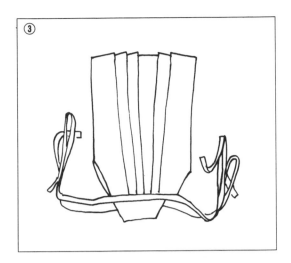

③ Turn the *hakama* over, taking care that the back part does not become disarranged. Pressing down on the hems while turning the *hakama* should help you keep a neat back. Arrange the three left-hand pleats and the two right-hand pleats.

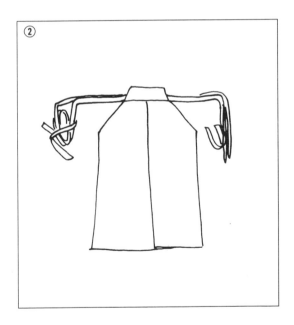

② Lay out the *hakama* face down on the floor with the rear center seam aligned on top of the front center seam. Smooth out any creases and align the hems.

④ Fold both sides inward approximately 10 cm.

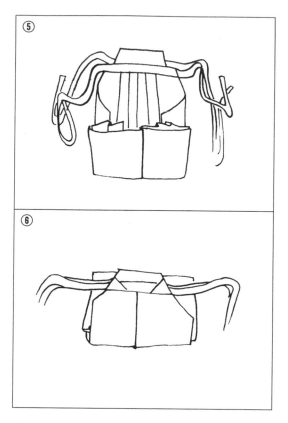

⑤⑥ Keeping a neat hem, fold the *hakama* into three from the hem side.

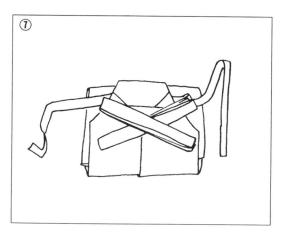

⑦ Fold the *mae-himo* (long strings) into four and cross over.

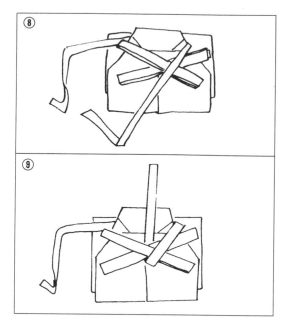

⑧⑨ Wind the *ushiro-himo* around the *mae-himo* from top to bottom, bringing it out above as shown in illustration ⑨. (The illustration shows the process beginning with the right *ushiro-himo*, but you may start from the left side if preferred.)

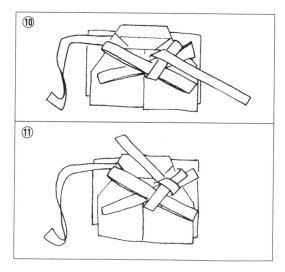

⑩⑪ Wind around the right-hand *mae-himo* from top to bottom, bringing it out above as shown in illustration ⑪.

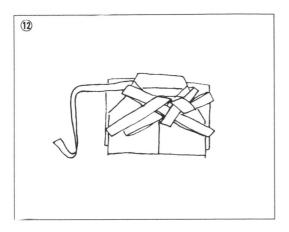

⑫ Lay over the right-hand *mae-himo* (now on the left-hand side of the *hakama*).

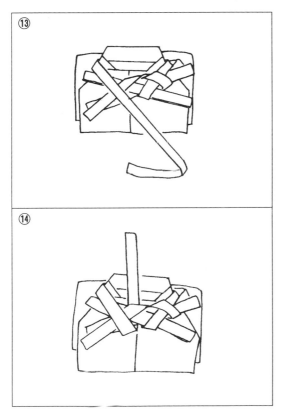

⑬⑭ Wind the left-hand *ushiro-himo* around the *mae-himo* from top to bottom, bringing it out above as shown in illustration ⑭.

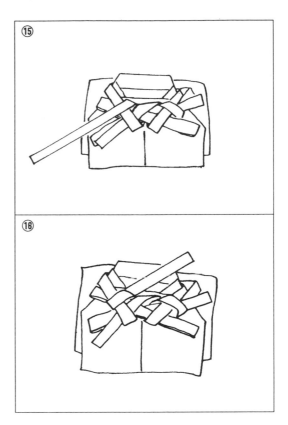

⑮⑯ Wind around the left-hand *mae-himo*, passing it underneath from the top, and bringing it out above as shown in illustration ⑯.

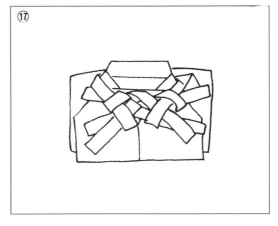

⑰ Bring toward the left *mae-himo* (now on the right-hand side), passing it underneath the right-hand *ushiro-himo*.

Putting on *Keiko-gi* and *Hakama*

A well-fitting *hakama* should hang just below the ankles. Both *hakama* and *keiko-gi* are made from extremely durable fabric and thus it makes sound economic sense for younger Kendoists to purchase a large *hakama* that can be easily altered. As shown in Fig. A below, sleeves are usually shortened from the shoulder and the height from the waist.

Failure to attend *keiko* with freshly-laundered and neatly-folded *hakama* and *keiko-gi* results in the crumpled and untidy example illustrated in Fig. B below. Treating all your Kendo equipment with appropriate care is an essential part of adopting the correct attitude to Kendo and a prerequisite to becoming a competent Kendoist.

Natural Posture

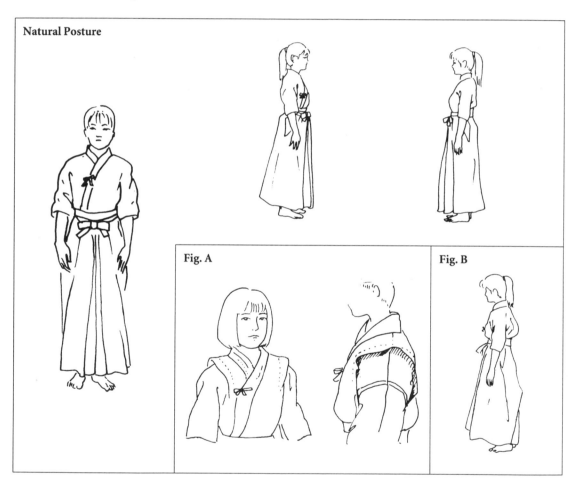

Fig. A

Fig. B

Length and Weight of the *Shinai*

The length and weight of the *shinai* varies according to the user as shown in the table below. The weight does not include the *tsuba* (sword guard). This is made of leather or an alternative synthetic material and is circular in shape, its diameter not exceeding 8 cm. The *tsuba* must be attached firmly to the *tsuka* (hilt).

When choosing a *shinai*, use the distance between the floor and your chest as a guide-line.

Shinai Standard

	Sex	12–15 years	15–18 years	Adult
Length	M/F	Max. 114 cm	Max. 117 cm	Max. 120 cm
Weight	M	Min. 425 g	Min. 470 g	Min. 500 g
	F	Min. 400 g	Min. 410 g	Min. 420 g

✳ In Japan, the length of the *shinai* to be used is determined by the age of the Kendo player, not the height.

Length of the *Tsuka*

The length of the *tsuka* should be such that when the tip is placed on the inside of the right elbow joint and the right elbow is bent to an angle of 90 degrees, there is no gap between the index finger and *tsuba*.

✳ People who use a long *tsuka* are often good at *ōji-waza* (counter-attacking techniques), while those who use a short one tend to strike from a longer *maai* (distance). The length of the *tsuka* is an important indicator of an opponent's habits.

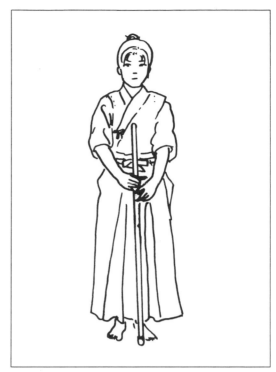

Chest height is the standard way of choosing the correct length of *shinai*

The standard way of measuring the length of the *tsuka*

Etiquette

Kendo involves putting on *kendōgu* and practicing with a partner, using a *shinai* to strike or thrust your partner on specified parts of the body. The relationship between you and your partner may be thought of as one in which each person discovers their own particular weak points through an exchange of strikes and thrusts. When you receive a strike, it should make you aware that you have a weak spot in that particular place.

Being on the receiving end of a strike, however, will inevitably make you feel disappointed and consequently *keiko* can turn quite rough. As a result, more *suki* (opening for attacks) will appear, causing you even more problems and leaving you open to even more strikes. You must always take care that this does not happen.

Paradoxically, successful Kendo depends on your ability to keep up a fighting spirit while continually showing appropriate respect to your partner. Your Kendo will become very unbalanced if one of these complementary elements is missing. We recommend strict observance of Kendo etiquette to help you make the most of *keiko*. Besides facilitating better practice, correct etiquette also gives rise to the beauty found in Kendo.

When you receive a strike, it is because there is a *suki*. Your opponent draws your attention to your weak spots, and you endeavor to ensure that you do not receive a strike in the same place again. Through endless repetition, the *suki* will gradually disappear. No one can ever rest on their laurels, however, even when they have reached the top level. In Kendo, there is always unlimited room for improvement.

Sitting, standing, and respectful behavior is formal etiquette. There is also "the etiquette of the heart," which is to approach Kendo with an open and frank attitude with the aim of self-improvement.

How to sit (when rising to a standing position from *seiza*, the procedure is reversed)

How to Sit and Stand

Kneel from Your Left Knee, and Rise from Your Right

① From an upright posture, place your right hand between your knees and divide your *hakama* to the left and right.

② Draw your left leg back and kneel on your left knee (with the tips of your toes perpendicular to the floor).

③ Draw your right leg back and kneel on both knees (with the tips of your toes perpendicular to the floor).

④ Lower your body to rest on your haunches, at the same time stretching your feet out straight behind (bringing the toes together, or overlapping them).

＊ The space between your knees should be equal to one or two clenched fists and your legs should be relaxed.

＊ Keep your back straight and relax your shoulders.

＊ Both hands should be placed flat on your upper thighs, fingers together.

＊ This is the correct posture to adopt when listening to the *sensei* (instructor) speak.

＊ Turn your face toward the *sensei* when he is not directly opposite you. Do not simply move your eyes.

＊ When rising to a standing position, this procedure is reversed.

Sitting Bow

① Assume the *seiza* position.

② Looking at your partner, place both hands together on the floor with your index fingers and thumbs touching to form a triangle.

③ Keeping your back straight, bend forward from the hips, taking care that the nape of your neck cannot be seen by your partner.

④ After taking one breath, raise the upper half of your body.

⑤ Looking at your partner, bring both hands back at the same time to rest on your upper thighs.

From Standing Bow to *Sonkyo* (Knee-bend Squat)—With Controlled Dignity

① Face your opponent with your shoulders and back straight (*sage-tō*).

Hold the *tsubamoto* lightly in your left hand, with your arm held by your side in a natural, relaxed way (the *tsuru* facing the floor).

② Keeping your eyes fixed on your partner, perform the standing bow to less than 15 degrees.

③ Bring the *shinai* to the left side of your waist, and place your thumb on the *tsuba* (with the *shinai* at an angle of 45 degrees).

Keeping your back straight, move forward from your right foot, with large, slow paces in a controlled and dignified manner.

④⑤⑥ On the third step, place your right thumb below the *tsuka* and grip the *shinai*. Draw the *shinai* with a large and open movement.

⑦ Lower yourself into the *sonkyo* position, in a slow and controlled manner.

Your back should be straight, and your abdominal muscles taut.

Sonkyo and Nōtō (Resheathing the Sword) Whether You Win or Lose, Always Keep Your Back Straight When Performing

① Perform *sonkyo* directly from *chūdan-no-kamae*, without shifting the position of your feet.

②③ Remove your left hand from the *tsuka* and with your right return the *shinai* beside your left thigh.

The *tsuru* should be facing the floor.

④ Place your left thumb on the *tsuba*.

⑤ Place your right hand on your upper thigh.

⑥ With the *shinai* held at your left side at waist height (*taitō*), rise to a standing position.

From your left foot, retreat five small steps, lower the *shinai* (*sage-tō*), and perform the standing bow.

* When the *shinai* is held at the *taitō* position, your thumb must always be placed on the *tsuba*.

* When the *shinai* is lowered to the *sage-tō* position, do not place your thumb on the *tsuba*.

* Some fail to abide by these rules when they lose. This is unacceptable. It is all the more important to adhere to form when you have lost.

In Kendo, the winner should always have a considerate and generous attitude toward the loser. This is what is meant by the spirit of fair play. Even more important is never to forget that the *dōjō* is the place which cultivates the kind of person who is able to congratulate the winner when he himself has lost. These congratulations are offered at the last standing bow.

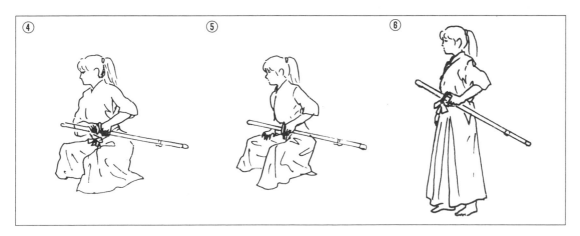

How to Hold the *Men, Kote,* and *Shinai* When Standing in a Line or Moving

When standing in a line or moving, the *kote* should be placed inside the *men* and fastened firmly with the *men-himo*. The *men* should be held so that the *kote* are visible. The *shinai* is held in the left hand. I would like to stress this, as there are those who move holding the *tsuki-dare*, or who do not fasten the *men-himo*, letting them trail along the floor. Others let their *kote* fall from inside the *men* and continue to move without realizing it. As the illustration shows, if the *men, kote,* and *shinai* are held correctly such things can be avoided

How to hold the *men, kote,* and *shinai* when standing in line or moving

Untie the *Men-himo* Resting the *Men* on Your Lap

When you have stopped moving and have sat down in position, place the *men* on your lap and untie the *men-himo*. As the *dōjō* floor is made of wood, it is liable to be scratched or marked if the *men* is placed there directly.

By ensuring that you hold the *men* correctly under your arm while standing, the *men-gane* (grill) will not come into direct contact with the floor. If you first place the *shinai* down on your left-hand side and bring the *men* to the front, it should naturally come to rest on your lap. If the *men-gane* comes into

contact with the floor, it means that you are not holding it correctly.

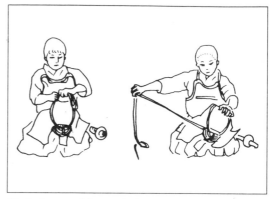

Untie the *men-himo* with the *men* resting on your lap

Put the *Shinai* Down So That the *Tsuba* Is Level with Your Kneecaps

This should be an almost silent action. If the *shinai* is put down in one movement, its whole length will come into contact with the floor. Noise is inevitable. We recommend a two-stage approach: put the tip of the *shinai* down gently and then bring the *tsuba* to rest on the floor. The *men* should be positioned approximately 20 cm in front and to one side of your right knee.

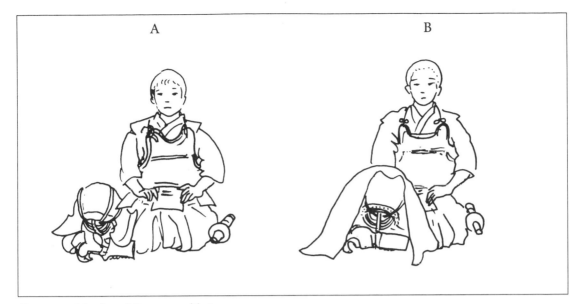

Correct positioning of the *men* and *kote*

Place the *Men* and *Kote* in Front and to the Side of Your Right Knee

The *kote* are placed horizontally, with the fists facing to the right, and the *men* on top. If the *kote* were arranged vertically, the *men* would not rest stable, and could fall, bringing the *men-gane* in contact with the floor.

As shown in the illustration below, correct positioning of the *men* and *kote* facilitates the sitting bow.

There are two ways of positioning the *tenugui*, as shown in illustrations A and B. Illustration A shows the *tenugui* folded neatly and placed inside the *men*. Illustration B shows the *tenugui* opened out and placed on top of the *men*. Both alternatives are acceptable.

The correct position of the *men* and *kote* for the sitting bow

Shizentai (Natural Standing Position) Is the Basis of *Kamae* (Guard Position)

Shizentai—a relaxed and stable standing position—should be well balanced with no unnecessary force applied. This posture will enable you to react swiftly and accurately in response to both your own movements and those of your partner.

- Feet should be placed slightly apart, with equal weight applied, and not leaning to one side.
- Knees should not be bent, nor completely straight, but relaxed.
- The back should be held upright, maintaining the natural curve of the spinal column; the abdomen should be held taut, and shoulders relaxed; the arms should hang naturally at the sides.

When the *shizentai* is maintained, it is supported by the muscles surrounding the spinal column. The maintenance of correct posture can be cultivated by first being aware of one's own posture in a mirror and observing it, so that eventually correct posture becomes a habit.

Chūdan-no-Kamae Should Be Relaxed and Dignified

Kamae is the stance of being ready at all times to react toward any changes in a partner's intentions. In Kendo, there are two types of *kamae*: that of the spirit and that of the body.

Kamae of the spirit (*kokoro-gamae*) is the state of being mentally and spiritually prepared to deal with things before they happen.

Kamae of the body (*mi-gamae*) is the posture adopted to move in and strike something that is coming in to attack. In Kendo, by firstly adopting *kamae* of the spirit, we are able to adopt correct *kamae* of the body. In other words, if *kamae* of the spirit is correct, correct *kamae* of the body will follow.

There are five *kamae*s for *tachi* in *Nihon Kendō-kata*: *jōdan-no-kamae* (upper guard position), *chūdan-no-kamae* (middle guard position), *gedan-no-kamae* (lower guard position), *hassō-no-kamae* (guard position with the *shinai* held vertically at one's right side), and *waki-gamae* (guard position having the *shinai* at one's side in order to conceal the arm). In present-day Kendo, *chūdan* and

Shizentai

Chūdan-no-kamae

jōdan are the principal *kamae*s. Only *chūdan* is explained here; *jōdan* and the other three *kamae*s are explained in Chapter 4—"Nihon Kendō-kata."

Chūdan-no-kamae

Chūdan-no-kamae enables you to react at will, whether for attack or defence, to any *kamae* you may be faced with.

- Basically, your left hand grips the *tsuka-gashira* (top of the hilt) and your right hand grips the *tsubamoto*.
- A *kamae* in which there is a gap between the right hand and the *tsuba* is lacking in dignity. This can be remedied by adjusting the length of the *tsuka*.
- The *tsuru* faces upward, and the *shinai* should be gripped from the top, so that the area between index finger and thumb of the left hand comes above the line of the *tsuru*.
- The *shinai* should be gripped with the middle, third, and little fingers of the left and right hands (with the little finger having the strongest grip), and the thumbs and index fingers should then rest lightly.

- The height of the *kensen*, held at an *issoku ittō no maai* (the distance at which one can attack, or avoid attack in one step), should be such that an imaginary line running out from the end of the *shinai* would reach your partner's throat. This is obviously variable.
- The left hand is placed at the center line of the body (so that an imaginary straight line running out from the base of the hand would pass through the navel and divide the body into two equal parts).
- The left hand should be positioned the distance of one clenched fist in front of and below the navel.
- The most important point to remember in *chūdan-no-kamae* is that the left hand acts as the fulcrum.

＊ Try using a *katana* (sword) or *bokutō* (wooden sword) for a clearer understanding of how to grip the *shinai*.

The Range of *Kensen* Movement—Upward and Downward, Left and Right

If the *kensen* is raised above the level of your partner's throat, power and intensity are lost. Further, if the *kensen* faces upward, the *kamae*

Upward/downward sweep of your partner's *shinai*   *Katsugi-waza*

becomes full of *suki*. The *kensen* and the state of your spirit are intimately connected, as is apparent from the following words from an old style of Kendo known as *Shintō Munenryū*: "The sword follows the hand, the hand follows the spirit."

You must also ensure that the *kensen* does not drop below the level of your partner's right *kote*. If you let it drop too low, your *kote* becomes vulnerable from above. There is also the chance that your *men* may be struck by *nidan-waza* from the *kote*.

The *kensen* should only move left and right within the limits of your partner's body.

In particular, when using such techniques as the upward sweep, downward sweep, and direct strike of your partner's *shinai*, it is easy for the *kensen* to face the outside of your partner's body. At such times it is better to perform these techniques using as small and sharp movements as possible. Also, techniques such as *katsugi-waza* ("shouldering-the-sword" technique) that necessarily involve moving the *kensen* away from your partner can only be successfully executed after you have overcome your partner with "*ki*."

＊ The Japanese word "*ki*" is an essential concept for the understanding of Kendo. It embodies the idea of a movement outward from the inner spirit, projecting itself in the form of a powerful energy, and is usual-

ly translated as "spirit" or "mental energy." Moreover, if the *kamae* of being able to strike at the appropriate moment is not maintained, then that opportunity will be missed. No matter how good posture appears to be from the outside, it cannot actually be so if an opportunity to strike is missed.

Study Your *Kamae* in the Mirror

There is a tendency for *chūdan-no-kamae*, no matter how carefully taught, to lapse during *keiko*. This can be checked by making a deliberate effort to stand in front of a mirror and study your *kamae* before *keiko*. The following points should be observed:

• What is the height of the *kensen*?

• How is your left hand positioned?

• What is the space between your left and right feet?

• What is the overall balance of your body, viewed from the side?

• When you swing the *shinai* upward, does it move in a straight line?

• When you swing the *shinai* downward, what is the position of your right hand? And your left?

Checking your *kamae* in this way and carrying it through to the next *keiko* is one part of *keiko* itself.

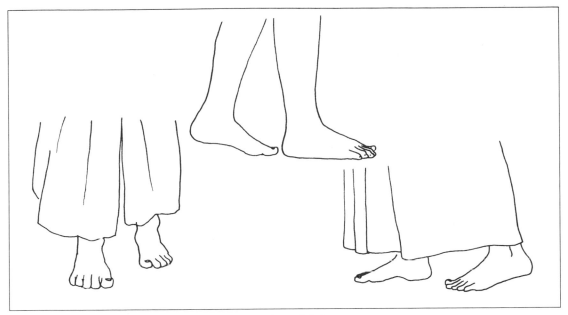

Kamae of the feet—the importance of the position of your left foot

Kamae of the Feet
The Importance of the Position of Your Left Foot

- Both feet should point forward in a straight line, with a gap of about 10 cm between them.

- The right foot should be forward, and the front of the left foot should be roughly level with the right heel.

- The left heel should be raised very slightly, so that the weight of the body falls evenly on both.

- Knees should neither be too tense, nor too relaxed.

- Both knees should always have a moderate amount of slack in the joints to facilitate movement at all times.

You should always take off from your left foot. Your left foot, therefore, should always be in the correct position to strike from a distance, take advantage of your partner's *suki*, and take off at precisely the right moment. Make sure that the gap between your feet is not too wide or your posture will collapse when you strike. And if your left foot faces outward, there is usually a corresponding loosening of guard.

It pays to keep an eye on the position of your left foot in Kendo.

Keep Your Left Knee Straight

If your left knee bends, it is because you have been overcome by your partner and succumbed to defeat. It is important to stand firm and, as a matter of form, not allow your left knee to bend. This does not mean that you should brace your leg, but rather that you should not succumb, not be timid. A strong-looking opponent, a very tall partner, or someone wearing splendid *kendōgu* can appear threatening even before a match has started. In the beginning the two Kendo players stand equal before one another, but as time progresses one becomes stronger and the other weaker.

This is because the more powerful is winning through "*ki*." Through the power of that *ki*, the weaker becomes timid and his left knee bends. It is important not to lose the battle between *ki* and *ki*, since the purpose of *keiko* may be said to be to "cultivate *ki*."

Ashi-sabaki (Footwork)

Okuri-ashi (sliding step with leading right foot)

Okuri-ashi is the most frequently used *ashi-sabaki* in *keiko*. When advancing, you move from the front foot; when retreating, you move with the rear foot. In *ashi-sabaki*, it is important that your movements be smooth, and that there be no movement of the body up and down or from side to side.

- *Okuri-ashi* is used to shorten or close the *maai*.

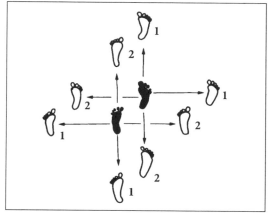

Okuri-ashi

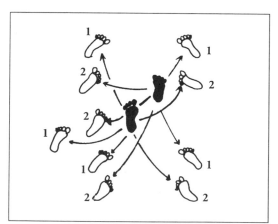

Hiraki-ashi

Hiraki-ashi (sideways step)

Hiraki-ashi is used when attacking your partner from one side, and when positioning your

feet in response to a strike. For example, *suriage-waza* (rising-slide deflection technique), *uchiotoshi-waza* (technique in which you strike down your partner's *shinai* in his attack and counterattack immediately), and *kaeshi-waza* (reflex-deflection technique) are three types of *waza* in which *hiraki-ashi* is used. At such times, it is essential that you face your partner squarely as you move.

Tsugi-ashi (short step)

Tsugi-ashi is used to shorten the distance between your feet, by drawing your left foot forward toward your stationary right foot. This is used when striking from a distance, enabling you to quickly shorten the distance between yourself and your partner.

Ayumi-ashi (walking step)

Ayumi-ashi is moving your left and right feet alternately, just as in the way you walk normally. This *ashi-sabaki* is used when you want to move quickly over a long distance, or by the *sensei* (or partner leading the practice) performing *kirikaeshi* (continuous strikes of right and left *men* alternately).

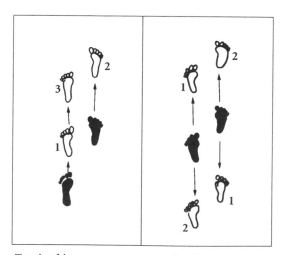

Tsugi-ashi   *Ayumi-ashi*

At the same time, it must be remembered that there are certain drawbacks to moving the left foot in front of the right. If you always move your left foot in front of the right to shorten the *maai* when striking from a distance, it can become a habit. If this tendency is not corrected at an early stage the situation develops where the beginner is unable to strike unless he adopts this *ashi-sabaki*. Care must be taken in this respect, because in *jigeiko* and matches the movement of the feet will alert the opponent to your intended strike.

Keep Your Toes Down in *Ashi-sabaki*

In *ashi-sabaki*, slide your feet along the floor without pointing your toes upward. This will enable you to move smoothly forward and back, left and right. If you move with your toes pointing upward, your movement will become awkward, and your partner will pick up on even the slightest error in your footwork and execute a strike.

Often after a strike, the player moves forward quickly with great energy, using *okuri-ashi*, and if large steps are taken his toes will turn upward. In fact, you have to point your toes upward in order to take a large step forward with the right foot. You should therefore make your step shorter, and move quickly.

Suri-ashi (sliding step) can be performed very easily on an unvarnished wood floor, but is difficult on surfaces that have been treated to prevent slipping.

A further example of toes pointing upward is when, after making a strike, the player relaxes and moves forward with *okuri-ashi*. *Ashi-sabaki* should be executed as far as possible moving with the lower back parallel to the floor.

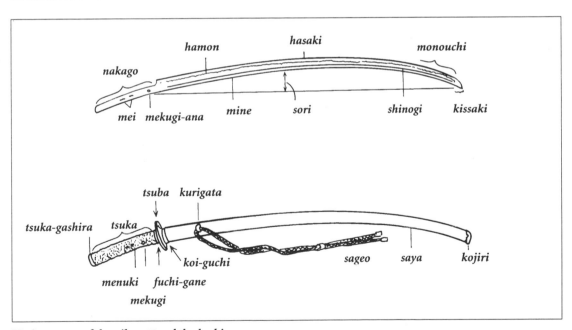

Various parts of the *nihon-tō* and the *koshirae*

How to Swing the *Shinai*

Manipulation of the *nihon-tō* is the basis of the Kendo strike or thrust. Since, however, the *shinai* is straight with a round cross-section, you cannot simply strike from any position you choose. As with the *nihon-tō*, when two *shinai*s strike each other the line of the cutting edge must carry right through. The practice of moving the *shinai* through space in this way is called *suburi*. There is a tendency to think of *suburi* as a warming-up exercise before *keiko* begins. This is a serious mistake, however, for if you cannot perform correct *suburi* then you will be unable to execute a correct strike. To perform correct *suburi*, swing the *shinai* in such a way that it travels to its target through the shortest possible distance.

For beginners, it is best to practice *suburi* by first standing in front of a mirror and swinging the *shinai* on the spot. Once able to do this correctly, beginners should proceed through the various stages toward coordination of arms and feet in accordance with *ashi-sabaki*.

Upward and Downward Swing

① Assume *chūdan-no-kamae*.

② Swing the *shinai* upward in a large movement, so that the *kensen* and right and left *kobushi* travel in a perfectly centered straight line.

③ Swing the *shinai* right back over your head, until the *kensen* reaches the center of your buttocks.

④ Swing the *shinai* forward and downward, so that it travels in a perfectly centered straight line.

⑤ Making sure that the *shinai* does not deviate from the center, swing it downward so that the *kensen* reaches approximately the height of your knees.

✳ Keep your shoulders and wrists relaxed.

✳ For ⑤, take care not to lean forward.

Upward and downward swing ①②③

Upward and downward swing ④⑤

Shōmen suburi ①

Shōmen (Center Men) Suburi

① Assume *chūdan-no-kamae*.

②③ Without changing the position or strength of your grip, swing the *shinai* upward and over your head in a large movement, so that the *kensen* and right and left *kobushi* travel in a perfectly centered straight line.

④ From the back, swing the *shinai* downward, so that it travels in a centered line.

⑤ Bring the *shinai* to rest with your right arm extended almost horizontally at shoulder level, and your left *kobushi* at chest level, and hold it in *tenouchi* (balance of strength of hands at the moment of strike or thrust: the grip on the *shinai* is tightened at the very last moment before striking).

✴ Repeated practice is necessary to master ⑤, the crucial element of *shōmen suburi*. For points ①②③ and ④, it is enough to remember not to grip the *shinai* too hard nor to let it fall. Between ② and ④ and up to the point immediately preceding ⑤, the *shinai* is swung forward and downward as if it were being thrown out. Finally, at the moment of ⑤, the grip on the *shinai* is tightened and then immediately relaxed.

✴ To begin with, practice *shōmen suburi* on the spot. Once you have got used to this, carry it out in combination with *ashi-sabaki*.

Kote (Forearm) Suburi

① Assume *chūdan-no-kamae*.

② Swing the *shinai* upward to the point where your partner's *kote* can be seen from below your left *kobushi*.

③ Swing the *shinai* downward so that it extends straight out at the level of your partner's *kote*, and hold it in *tenouchi*.

✴ Swing the *shinai* downward until it is almost parallel with the floor.

✴ Your eyes should be directed straight ahead.

✴ To begin with, practice *kote suburi* on the spot; once you have got used to this, carry it out in combination with *ashi-sabaki*.

Left Men Suburi

① Assume *chūdan-no-kamae*.

② Swing the *shinai* up in a centered straight line to the point where your partner's *men* can be seen from below your left *kobushi*.

③ Adjusting the position of your right hand, swing the *kensen* downward from the

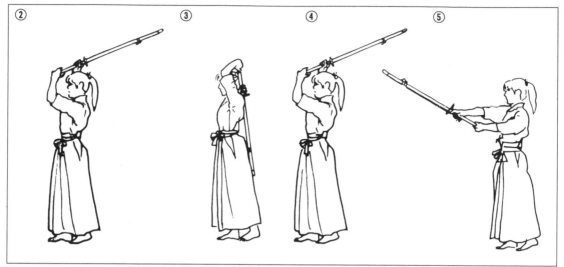

Shōmen suburi ②③④⑤

right at an angle of 30–45 degrees toward your partner's left *men*.

④ Holding the *shinai* in *tenouchi*, bring the *kensen* to rest at your partner's left *men*.

✳ Check the angle of the downward swing.

✳ The left *kobushi* should be straight and centered.

Right *Men Suburi*

① Assume *chūdan-no-kamae*.

② Swing the *shinai* upward in a centered straight line to the point where your partner's *men* can be seen from below your left *kobushi*.

③ Adjusting the position of your right hand, swing the *kensen* downward from the left at an angle of 30–45 degrees, toward your partner's right *men*.

Kote suburi

Left *men suburi*

④ Holding the *shinai* in *tenouchi*, bring it to rest at your partner's right *men*.

* The left *kobushi* should be straight and centered.

* When left and right *men suburi* are repeated alternately, we call it "*renzoku sayū men suburi*" (continuous left and right *men suburi*). The upward swing follows the same path as the downward swing, and hand positions are adjusted when the *shinai* is held above the head, so that it comes down to rest at your partner's *men*. This can be easily understood by striking a continuous left and right *men* on your partner.

Left *Dō Suburi*

① Assume *chūdan-no-kamae*.

② Swing the *shinai* upward in a centered straight line to the point where your part-

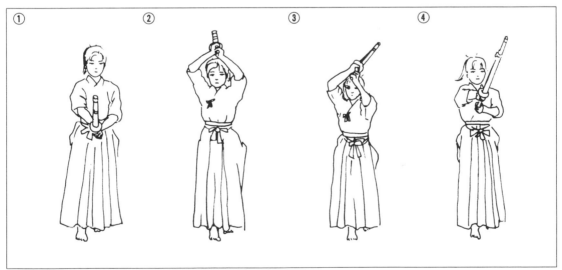

Right *men suburi*

Left *dō suburi*

ner's *dō* can be seen from below your left *kobushi*.

③ Adjusting the position of your right hand, swing the *kensen* downward from the right at an angle of approximately 45 degrees, toward your partner's left *dō*.

④ Holding the *shinai* in *tenouchi*, bring the *kensen* to rest at your partner's left *dō*.

✳ The right *kobushi* should be straight and centered.

Right *Dō Suburi*

① Assume *chūdan-no-kamae*.

② Swing the *shinai* upward in a centered straight line to the point where your partner's *men* can be seen from below your left *kobushi*.

③ Adjusting the position of your right hand, swing the *kensen* diagonally from the left at an angle of approximately 45 degrees, toward your partner's right *dō*.

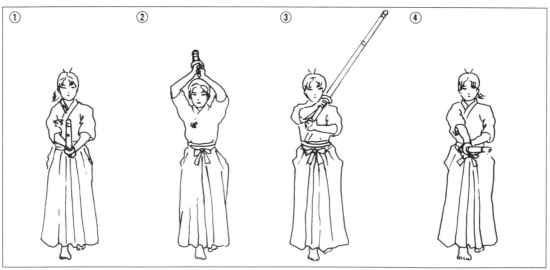

Right *dō suburi*

Chōyaku (jumping) *suburi*

④ Holding the *shinai* in *tenouchi*, bring the *kensen* to rest at your partner's right *dō*.

✳ The left *kobushi* should be straight and centered.

✳ When left and right *dō suburi* are repeated alternately, we call it "*renzoku sayū dō suburi*" (continuous left and right *dō suburi*). The upward swing follows the same path as the downward swing, and hand positions are adjusted when the *shinai* is held above the head, so that it comes down to rest at your partner's *dō*.

Chōyaku (Jumping) Suburi

① From *chūdan-no-kamae*, swing the *shinai* straight up in a large movement.

② As your left foot is thrown back and kicks the floor, spring forward with your right foot, swinging the *shinai* sharply down, bringing it to rest with your right arm at shoulder level and your left *kobushi* at chest level.

• The left foot should quickly follow the right.

③ As your right foot is thrown back and kicks the floor, spring back with your left foot, and swing the *shinai* up in a large movement.

• The right foot should quickly follow the left.

④ As in ②.

✳ When you spring forward, ensure that your left foot is not brought down in front of your right.

✳ When you spring back with a large movement, ensure that your hands and feet are coordinated.

✳ Beginners should perform this slowly, and gradually increase speed as progress is made.

✳ Beginners' progress can be measured by their ability to perform *chōyaku suburi*. A particularly important part of *keiko* is to cultivate the power of backward kicking at the same time as swinging the *shinai* in order to kick back with the left foot and strike the opponent. This backward kicking action is similar to that of the right foot of a runner taking off at the start of a race.

✳ The technique of *kote-nuki-men* may be said to be an application of *chōyaku suburi*.

Maai

Maai refers to the distance between you and your partner. In a broad sense, it designates the spatial aspect, but the word "*ma*" also includes the idea of seizing the chance, or of timing.

Ma is often said to be the most important aspect of Kendo. Although the different *maai* can be described in terms of form, as below, when it comes to *keiko* or matches they are often elusive and difficult to grasp. There is *ma* which can be taught, therefore, and *ma* which cannot be taught.

Issoku Ittō no Maai

This is the distance which enables you to strike your partner from *ai-chūdan* (both partners in *chūdan-no-kamae*) by taking only one step forward. It is also the *maai* which enables you to avoid a strike from your partner by taking only one step backward. Broadly speaking, it is the distance required to cross your *shinai* with that of your partner at a point approximately 10 cm from the *kensen*.

∗ This varies according to age, sex, strength, ability, build, length of *shinai*, opportuni-ty to strike, etc. This is the *ma* which cannot be taught, but rather which we have to learn by ourselves through *keiko*.

Tōma

This *maai* designates a longer distance than *issoku ittō*. When in this *maai* you can neither receive nor administer a strike. When you wish to strike from this *maai* you must first move into *issoku ittō no maai*.

Beginners should perform *keiko* from *tōma* with skillful *ashi-sabaki* that includes the backward kicking action. When *keiko* is performed from *tōma*, it cultivates an ability to become less self-conscious as well as developing muscles used in Kendo. For beginners to make progress it is particularly important that they do not focus too much on the *kote-saki* from *chikama* (close distance), but perform *keiko* with large and relaxed movements using their whole body.

Issoku ittō no maai

Tōma

Chikama

This designates a distance closer than *issoku ittō no maai*. In this *ma* it is easy to strike your partner, but just as easy to receive a strike. When striking from *chikama, waza* (techniques) become small, and there is little need to kick back with your left foot. For beginners, it is important to strike with a large movement and from a long distance.

Chikama

A difference in height between two partners will alter *maai*

The illustration shows the *maai* and level of the *kensens* where a difference in height exists between two partners:

Ⓐ is a male, 135 cm tall
Ⓑ is a female, 155 cm tall

As explained in the section on *issoku ittō no maai*, Kendo is influenced by the age, sex, strength, ability, and build of the players, the length of the *shinai*, etc., yet we all perform *keiko* together in the same *dōjō* or gym. You may find that your partner in *keiko* or your opponent in a match is over 180 cm tall, or around 150 cm tall. The psychological effects of such a situation are significant in that they influence the kind of *maai* we adopt. Tall opponents must not despise smaller ones and smaller opponents must not be afraid of tall ones. Rather, *maai* and the level of the *kensen* need to be more flexible at these times.

∗ As a guideline for the height of the *kensen*, an imaginary line running from the tip should reach your partner's throat area.

Tsubazeriai

Sometimes, you will move in extremely close to your partner so that the *tsubamotos* of your *shinai*s make contact. This is called *tsubazeriai*. The *shinai*s are crossed at a very sharp angle, and the *tsubamotos* are locked together.

From this *maai* you can strike your partner by breaking his posture, or respond to your partner's strike as he steps back by moving forward and executing a strike. In this situation, *hiki-waza* (stepping back technique) is important. *Keiko* must therefore be performed using both the *waza* of moving forward and executing a strike, and moving backward and executing a strike.

Tsubazeriai

Standing Bow at Nine Paces

The standing bow should be performed at a *maai* of nine paces. Each player should then advance three paces and adopt the *sonkyo* position. The *kensen*s should not come into contact at this time.

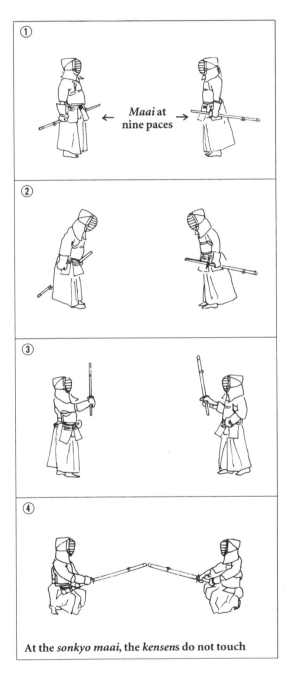

①
Maai at nine paces ←→

②

③

④

At the *sonkyo maai*, the *kensen*s do not touch

The *metsuke* (point of observation) is directed toward your partner's whole body.

In Kendo, great emphasis is placed on eye movement. The best words to describe this are "*enzan no metsuke*" (fixing one's eyes on a distant mountain). This means that you should not focus your eyes on one point; rather, you should focus on the body as a whole, taking your partner's eyes as a central point. This will enable you to see not only physical movement but also any movement in your partner's mind. In its most extreme form, *metsuke* means actually being able to read your partner's mind, and is referred to by Miyamoto Musashi in his *Book of Five Rings* as the "*kan-ken no metsuke.*" This is normally nigh on impossible, but success will bring victory every time. To set yourself against this impossible challenge is what it means to perform *keiko*.

Metsuke is to look at your partner's whole body

How to Execute and Receive a Strike

Shōmen-uchi (center *men* strike)

① The player receiving the strike takes up a *maai* that will enable his partner to strike easily, moves his *shinai* so that the *kensen* points to the right, and offers *men*.

② The player executing the strike jumps forward at the precise moment *men* is offered and strikes *shōmen*.

- The player receiving the strike should remain directly facing his partner, and allow himself to receive the *shōmen* strike fully. He should then move to the right (or sometimes to the left) to enable his partner to advance directly forward.

Migi-kote-uchi (strike to the right forearm)

① The player receiving the strike takes up a *maai* that will enable his partner to strike easily, moves his *shinai* so that the *kensen* points to the left, and offers *migi-kote*.

- If your hand is raised slightly, it will make it easier for your partner to strike.

② The player executing the strike jumps forward at the precise moment *migi-kote* is offered and strikes *migi-kote*.

Migi-dō-uchi (strike to the right trunk)

① The player receiving the strike takes up a *maai* that will enable his partner to strike, and swings his *shinai* up, exposing *dō*.

② The player executing the strike jumps forward at the precise moment *dō* is offered and strikes *migi-dō*.

③④ The player executing the strike then advances quickly forward to the right.

How to receive a *shōmen* strike

How to receive a *kote* strike

How to receive a *migi-dō* strike ① ②

How to receive a *migi-dō* strike ③④

Kirikaeshi

Kirikaeshi refers to the continuous striking of left and right *men* alternately, and its *keiko* should be neglected by neither beginners nor black belts. When carried out correctly, *kirikaeshi* will foster physical strength, spirit, and vigor.

Method

① From *tōma*, give a loud shout and boldly strike *shōmen*.

②③ After *taiatari* (body check), swing the *shinai* up in a large movement and, beginning with left *men*, strike alternate left and right *men* 5, 7, or 9 times. Then move quickly from *tōma* to *chūdan*, and boldly strike *shōmen* immediately. This process should then be repeated.

✳ Strike left and right *men* correctly, while shouting "*men, men, men*" in a loud voice.

✳ Raise your *shinai* high over your head each time in a large and fully extended movement.

✳ If you try to perform this too quickly, you will fail to execute a correct strike.

✳ After the strike, your right *kobushi* should not diverge from a centered straight line.

✳ Perform *kirikaeshi* continuously, 30, 50, or 100 times.

✳ Strike continuously in the same breath.

✳ Instead of *sayū-men*, strike *sayū-dō* (left and right *dō*).

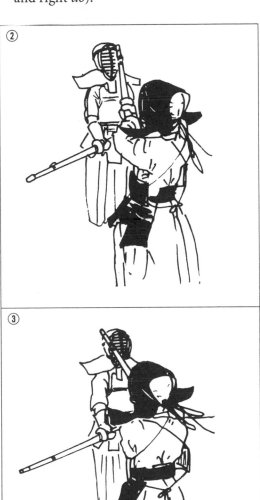

Foster physical strength, spirit, and vigor through *kirikaeshi*

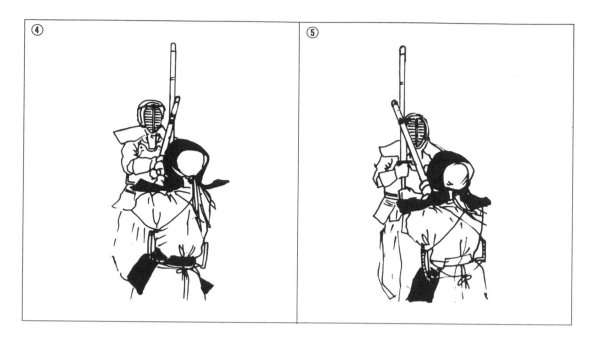

Points to Observe When Doing *Kirikaeshi*

* Keep your shoulders relaxed.

* After the strike, extend your right elbow.

* Perform *ashi-sabaki* correctly when moving forward and backward.

* Strike correctly with the cutting edge, avoiding *hirauchi* (strike with the flat of the *shinai*).

* As shown in illustrations ④ and ⑤, even if the teacher receives the strike with the *shinai*, the player should strike left and right *men* correctly with *monouchi* (see illustrations ⑥ and ⑦).

The Beneficial Effects of *Kirikaeshi*

1. Improves posture.
2. Improves breathing.
3. The strike becomes strong and reliable.
4. The shoulder joints become flexible.
5. Develops the skill of *tenouchi*.
6. Facilitates arm movement.
7. Posture becomes firm and solid.
8. Improves *ashi-sabaki*.

9. The appropriate *ma* for executing a strike is made clear.

10. Develops correct use of the cutting edge.

Excellent for restoring confidence lost during *keiko* or matches, *kirikaeshi* confers many other beneficial effects.

How to Receive *Kirikaeshi*

Beginners should allow themselves to be struck on the left and right *men* as shown in illustrations ② and ③. It is important to think of *kirikaeshi* as being the striking of left and right *men*, not as the striking of your partner's *shinai*.

Receiving with the *Shinai*

When receiving *kirikaeshi* with the *shinai*, you should hold the *shinai* vertically in front of your left and right *men* alternately, and use *tenouchi* to shield against your partner's *shinai*.

* Beginners should receive in such a way that *kirikaeshi* can be carried out without any obstruction.

* *Ayumi-ashi* is the appropriate *ashi-sabaki*.

⑥

Strike with *monouchi*

⑦

* *Kirikaeshi* is always led by the the player receiving strikes.

The Beneficial Effects of Receiving *Kirikaeshi*

1. Improves posture.
2. Facilitates movement.
3. When your partner strikes, the cutting edge becomes clear.
4. *Maai* becomes clear.
5. Develops *shinai* grip in *tenouchi*.

Kihon-Uchi (Basic Strike) with *Uchikomi Bō* (Attacking Exercise Stick)

When performing *shōmen-uchi keiko* with the *uchikomi-bō*, care must be taken to ensure the length of the stick is adjusted to suit the player's height. With two *uchikomi-bō*s, you can do *kote-men uchi* and *men-men uchi*. The difficult part is for the player to judge the correct *maai*.

Renzoku-Uchi (Continuous Strikes) with the *Shinai*

Ten, fifteen, or even more players can line up in a large *dōjō*. The space between A and B should be *tōma no maai*.

The player executing the strike gives a loud shout, swings up the *shinai*, and performs *renzoku-uchi* in one breath.

* * With each strike hold the *shinai* in *tenouchi* and strike firmly.
* * Do not allow your left foot to protrude in front of your right.
* * If you do not move your left foot forward quickly you will lean forward.
* * After the last strike, maintain *zanshin* (positive follow through of strike) and position yourself behind C.

Learn the Correct Amount of Force to Apply during a Strike with the *Uchikomi-dai* (1)

The horizontal pole moves according to the amount of force applied in the strike. After the strike, move forward quickly with *suri-ashi* to avoid the horizontal pole. If your strike is too light, the horizontal pole moves only slightly and will strike your face. On the other hand if your strike is too forceful, the pole comes back too quickly and will again strike your face. This makes the *uchikomi-dai* an effective method of *keiko* and enables you to learn the correct amount of force to apply during a strike.

Keiko with *uchikomi-dai* (1)

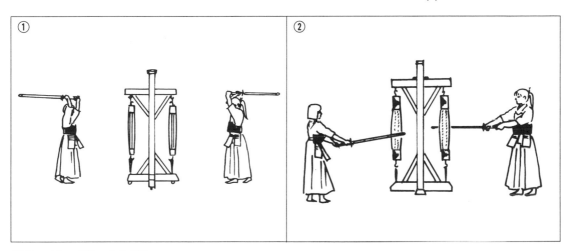

Keiko with *uchikomi-dai* (2)

Learn the Height of the Upward Swing and *Tenouchi* with the *Uchikomi-dai* (2)

Stand on the spot and perform *kirikaeshi* at *sayū-men* and *sayū-dō* height. This *keiko* teaches you to make a large, upward swing of the *shinai*, to hold the *shinai* in *tenouchi* as you strike, and to prevent leaning forward.

Look straight ahead, not at the point which is being struck.

* Four players can carry this out at the same time.

* It is entirely up to the individual how many times to practice this *keiko*.

Chapter

STRETCHING EXERCISES FOR KENDO

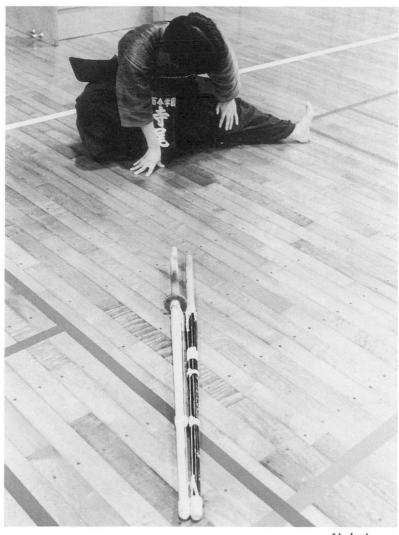

Limbering up

Stretching Before and After *Keiko*

Before *keiko*, a warming up session is necessary to ease any stiffness in the muscles, increase the efficiency of the organs, and prevent injury. Correct stretching loosens the muscles, facilitates movement, and leaves us feeling refreshed.

Stretching must be carried out in accordance with the muscle composition and flexibility of the individual and with varying levels of muscle tension. We should not push, bend, and stretch ourselves to the limit, since to do so will result in injury. The most important point is that the purpose of stretching is to relax mind and body.

❋ We should also carry out stretching after *keiko* to cool down and relax the mind and body.

Reasons for stretching:

1. To reduce muscle tension and maximize relaxation;
2. To increase movement of joints;
3. To prevent injury;
4. To send a signal to the muscles that we want to move;
5. To reduce psychological tension;
6. To stimulate the circulation.

Advice on stretching:

1. Stretch comfortably and hold for 10–30 seconds.
2. Do not apply force.
3. While stretching, breathe slowly and naturally.
4. Learn the best method to suit your own body.
5. When stretching your left and right sides, make sure that each side receives an equal amount of time.

Backs of Thighs and Lower Back

Stretch the back of your right thigh and the left side of your lower back:

- Sit on the floor with your left leg bent. Extend your right leg straight out.
- Lean forward from your lower back.
- Hold this position for approximately 20–30 seconds.

❋ Bend from the lower back.

❋ Relax shoulders and arms.

❋ Do not try to touch your toes by force.

❋ Repeat with left leg.

Insides of Thighs and Hips

Stretch the insides of your thighs and your hips:

- Sit with legs apart without exerting any force.
- Lean slowly forward from your lower back.
- Relax the quadriceps (thighs) and point your feet upward.
- Hold this position for approximately 20–30 seconds.

❋ You may place your hands in front of your body to keep your balance if desired.

❋ Do not try to touch your toes by force.

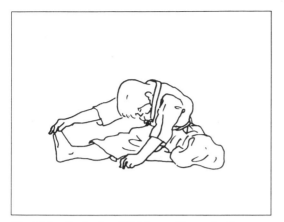

Stretching the backs of thighs and lower back

Stretching the backs of knees

Backs of Knees

Stretch the backs of your knees:

- Extend your right leg and bend your left leg on top. (The left leg should rest on the right thigh and not on the right knee.)
- Bend slowly forward from your lower back.
- Hold this position for approximately 20–30 seconds.

* Particularly effective for those with stiff knees.
* Do not try to touch your toes by force.
* Repeat with left leg.

Ankles

Stretch your ankles:

- Applying light pressure with your hands, rotate your ankle clockwise, then anti-clockwise.
- Rotate in both directions 10–20 times.
- Rotate the same number of times for both ankles.

* Rotating your ankles softly stretches hardened ligaments.
* Essential to prevent sprains during Kendo.
* Repeat with other ankle.

Stretching the insides of thighs and hips

Ankle stretching

Stretching arms, shoulders, and upper back

Arms, Shoulders, and Upper Back

- Stretch arms, shoulders, and upper back.
- Raise your arms above your head and interlock the fingers of both hands.
- With palms facing upward, push your arms slightly back and upward.
- Hold this position for approximately 15–20 seconds.

✳ Breathe naturally.

✳ Particularly effective in Kendo because we use our shoulder joints a lot during the upward and downward swings of the *shinai*.

Shoulders and Upper Back

Stretch your shoulders and the central upper back region:

- Bring one arm across the front of your chest and gently pull your elbow toward the opposite shoulder.
- Hold this position for approximately 10–15 seconds.

✳ Repeat with other arm.

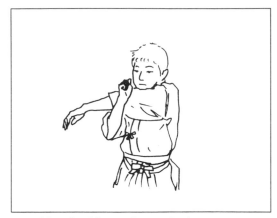

Stretching shoulders and upper back

Triceps and Shoulders

Stretch the triceps and the top of the shoulders:

- Raise both arms above your head, grasp one elbow, and stretch by pulling your elbow gently in the direction of your head.
- Do this slowly, holding this position for approximately 10–20 seconds.

✳ Particularly effective for easing the stiffness in arms and shoulders.

✳ The top right illustration on the next page shows the position from behind.

✳ Repeat with other arm.

Stretching triceps and shoulders

Arms, Shoulders, and Chest

Stretch your arms, shoulders, and chest:

- Clasp the fingers of both hands behind and slowly raise your arms.
- Expand your chest and brace your jaw.
- Hold this position for approximately 10–15 seconds.

✳ Particularly effective when the front of your shoulders are tired.

Shoulders

Stretch your shoulders:

- Bring both hands behind your body and if possible hold this position with your fingers hooked together. (Even if your fingers do not touch, you should still experience a considerable amount of stretching.)
- Hold this position for approximately 10–15 seconds.

✳ Stretch within your own personal limits. On no account force your fingers to touch or to hook together.

✳ Relieves tension in the muscles and improves flexibility.

✳ Particularly effective in revitalizing the upper half of the body.

✳ Repeat on opposite side.

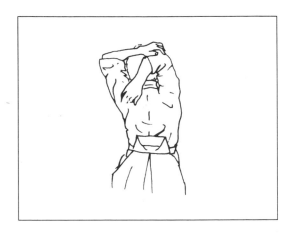

Stretching arms, shoulders, and chest

Stretching shoulders

Upper Body and Back

Stretch your upper body and back:

- Place your hands on the *dōjō* wall, shoulder-width apart, and bend your body forward and downward, with your knees slightly bent.

- Particularly effective for those who suffer from stiffness in the upper back or shoulders.

- Hold this position for approximately 20 seconds.

Stretching upper body and back

Calf Muscles

Stretch your calf muscles:

- Bend one leg and place the foot of that leg forward.

- Extend the other leg behind.

- Slowly move your hips forward, without twisting.

- Hold this position for approximately 20 seconds.

* Make sure that the heel of the foot which is extended behind remains in contact with the floor.

* The tips of your toes should face straight forward or slightly inward.

* Repeat with other leg.

Stretching calf muscles

Chapter

❸

WAZA (TECHNIQUES)

Waza practice

Waza Included in This Book

(1) *Shikake-waza*

1. *Tobikomi-men*
2. *Tobikomi-kote*
3. *Tobikomi-dō*
4. *Hikibana-kote*
5. *Katsugi-kote*

(*Nidan-waza*)
6. *Kote-men*
7. *Kote-dō*
8. *Men-dō*

(*Harai-waza*)
9. *Harai-age-men* (*omote**)
10. *Harai-age-men* (*ura***)
11. *Harai-kote* (*ura*)
12. *Harai-otoshi-men* (*omote*)

(*Debana-waza*)
13. *Debana-men*
14. *Debana-kote*

(2) *Ōji-waza*

(*Nuki-waza*)
15. *Men-nuki-dō*
16. *Kote-nuki-men*
17. *Kote-nuki-kote*

(*Suriage-waza*)
18. *Men-suriage-men* (*ura*)
19. *Men-suriage-men* (*omote*)
20. *Kote-suriage-men* (*ura*)
21. *Kote-suriage-kote*

(*Uchiotoshi-waza*)
22. *Dō-uchiotoshi-men*
23. *Kote-uchiotoshi-men*

(*Kaeshi-waza*)
24. *Men-kaeshi-dō*
25. *Kote-kaeshi-men*
26. *Kote-kaeshi-kote*

(3) *Tsubazeriai* and *Waza* from *Tsubazeriai*

(*Shikake-waza/Hiki-waza*)
27. *Hiki-men* from *tsubazeriai*
28. *Hiki-dō* from *tsubazeriai*
29. *Hiki-kote* from *tsubazeriai*

(*Ōji-waza*)
30. *Suriage-men* in response to *hiki-men* from *tsubazeriai* (*ura*)
31. *Suriage-men* in response to *hiki-men* from *tsubazeriai* (*omote*)
32. *Uchiotoshi-men* in response to *hiki-men* from *tsubazeriai* (*ura*)
33. *Uchiotoshi-men* in response to *hiki-men* from *tsubazeriai* (*omote*)
34. *Uchiotoshi-men* in response to *hiki-dō* from *tsubazeriai*
35. *Uchiotoshi-men* in response to *hiki-kote* from *tsubazeriai*

*   *Omote* refers to the left-side of the *shinai* when held correctly.

** *Ura* refers to the right-side of the *shinai* when held correctly.

Kendo *waza* (techniques) are broadly divided into two categories: *shikake-waza* (techniques to initiate a strike) and *ōji-waza* (techniques used in response to an attempted strike). In this book I have used three categories: (1) *shikake-waza*, (2) *ōji-waza*, and (3) *tsubazeriai* and *waza* from *tsubazeriai* (*shikake-waza*, *ōji-waza*). All three categories are explained from the *chūdan* position.

(1) *Shikake-waza*

Techniques used to create a *suki* in an opponent by initiating an attack, or to strike boldly when your opponent has himself created a *suki*. The most important point about *shikake-waza* is *sutemi* (acting without being too self-conscious).

1. *Tobikomi-waza*

Techniques used when an opponent shows weak *kisei* (spirit, vigor) or when he yields a *suki* under pressure from your own *kisei*. Remember to maintain your *kisei* and strike swiftly.

2. *Hikibana-waza*

It is a fact, that when attacked or about to make a strike, both body and *shinai* will lose balance. The *hikibana-waza* uses this momentary imbalance to facilitate the execution of a strike. Particular care should be taken when on the attack as your opponent is likely to employ this technique as he retreats or straightens his back.

3. *Katsugi-waza*

A technique that will provide a surprise attack achieved by lifting the *shinai* over your shoulder before striking. Note that skillful wielding of the *kensen* and a vigorous and spirited attack are essential for effective *katsugi-waza*.

4. *Nidan-waza*

There are two types of *nidan-waza*: 1) techniques for moving to the next *waza* after an unsuccessful first strike, and 2) techniques in which the first strike attracts and holds your opponent's concentration and physical posture, thus creating a *suki* to enable a successful second strike.

With the former, a continuous rhythm of correctly executed strikes is crucial. For the latter, make sure you execute the *waza* continuously, taking full advantage of your opponent's *suki*. It is also worth remembering that if a successful strike is not executed in *nidan* (two stages), the process may be repeated a third or fourth time, or even beyond, until a valid strike is executed.

5. *Harai-waza*

Effective technique when an opponent's *kamae* provides no *suki* in which to strike, employed at the moment an opponent moves to attack or begins to retreat. Involves sweeping up your opponent's *shinai* from below or knocking it down from above. A strike executed after the sweeping action must coincide exactly with the moment your opponent's *kamae* is broken.

6. Debana-waza

A *waza* used to execute a strike the moment you realize that your opponent is about to administer a strike himself. Your opponent's concentration will inevitably be focused on his strike and his posture will lack the necessary flexibility to respond quickly. An ideal opportunity to try a *debana-waza*. Note that if you score the first point with *debana-waza* in a three-strike match, your opponent will be unlikely to recover and so the outcome is likely to be in your favor.

(2) Ōji-waza

A technique used to execute a strike in response to an attempted strike by your opponent. Rather than wait for your opponent to strike, it is important to force a strike through aggressive attack and then play an *ōji-waza*.

1. Nuki-waza

Quite simply, *nuki-waza* involves moving yourself out of the way before your opponent moves in to strike. Timing is vital, for if you are too quick or too slow you will not be successful. Close observation of your opponent's movements is essential.

2. Suriage-waza

When struck by your opponent's *shinai*, this *waza* is used to sweep up his *shinai* in a rising-slide motion, using the left (*omote*) or right (*ura*) side of your *shinai*, and then to strike promptly in the direction of the opponent's *shinai*, or alternatively at the *suki* that will arise from the inevitable collapse of his composure. Make sure that the rising-slide motion and the upward-sweeping motion do not become separated into two stages, with the upward sweep changing suddenly into a rising slide; the motion is in effect an upward slide, smooth and unbroken.

3. Uchiotoshi-waza

When an opponent is about to strike, this technique knocks down his *shinai* to the right or left, rendering the strike ineffective, and at the same time providing you with an opportunity to strike. For this *waza* it is important to ascertain precisely your opponent's *maai* and to knock down his *shinai* before his arm is fully extended.

4. Kaeshi-waza

This technique responds to an opponent's attempted strike by warding off his attacking *shinai*, immediately flipping over your wrists and executing a strike to his opposite side.

(3) Tsubazeriai and Waza from Tsubazeriai

Techniques used to create a *suki* in your opponent by upsetting his balance, whereupon you step back promptly. Remember to: 1) use your opponent's strength against him when you strike; 2) from *tsubazeriai*, establish a comfortable striking distance; 3) move fast and strike firmly from your wrists because at this *maai* there is little room to build up momentum; 4) take care not to lose any *kisei* when you strike; 5) keep all *waza* sharp and accurate.

An *ōji-waza* can be an effective response to an ambivalent *hiki-waza* from *tsubazeriai* that is performed without appropriate *kisei*. Strict concentration is therefore a key element in *tsubazeriai*.

To be able to strike *hiki-waza* from this position increases the scope of your *keiko* and also gives you an advantage over an opponent who cannot.

It is a mistake to think that *hiki-waza* can only be performed from *tsubazeriai*. Its benefits can also be reaped when your opponent is obviously lacking confidence: upset his balance and use *hiki-waza* to follow with a swift and sure strike.

Criteria for *waza* described in this publication:

1. This publication includes all the categories covered in *Kendō-shidō-no-tebiki*, a manual edited by the Japanese Ministry of Education for high-school Kendo. I have also included the basic *men-uchi*, *kote-uchi*, and *dō-uchi* as *shikake-waza* because Kendo is fundamentally about personal attack and defense and I believe it is more valuable to perform *keiko* of even the most basic techniques with an awareness that your partner is in fact your opponent.

2. The manual does not refer to *hiki-waza* in great detail. Here, I have described some of the counters or *ōji-waza* that can used against *hiki-waza* performed from the *tsubazeriai*.

3. Also included are a number of *waza* not explained in the manual but common in actual *keiko* or matches, such as *katsugi-kote*, *kote-nuki-kote*, *kote-uchiotoshi-men*, *kote-kaeshi-men*, and *kote-kaeshi-kote*.

4. *Harai-waza* have been divided into two sections: *harai-age* and *harai-otoshi*. I have also made a distinction between the upward-sweeping techniques of *harai-ageru* with the right side of the *shinai* (*ura*) and *harai-ageru* with the left side of the *shinai* (*omote*), and the downward-sweeping technique of *harai-otosu*.

5. Finally, strange as this may sound, I believe that beginners should not rely too much on *waza*, since their *keiko* will become passive and their vigor will diminish. I would like to stress, therefore, that over and above *waza* the most important thing in Kendo is a vigorous fighting spirit.

(1) *Shikake-waza*

1. *Tobikomi-men*

① From *chūdan-no-kamae*, both players push forward to establish an *issoku ittō no maai*.

② Swing up the *shinai* in a large, swift movement until you can see the strike target (in this case, the *men*) between your raised arms.

③ As you throw your left foot back, take a large stride forward with your right foot and swiftly swing down the raised *shinai*.

④ As your right foot hits the floor, hold the *shinai* in *tenouchi* and strike your opponent's *men* accurately with the *monouchi*.

Tobikomi-men ①

Upward swing—basic technique to swing up the *shinai* until the strike target becomes visible between the player's raised arms.

Monouchi—one third of the *shinai* measured from the *kensen* (approximately 10 cm/4 inches in length).

Tobikomi-men ②③④

From top left, *tobikomi-kote* ①②③④

2. Tobikomi-kote

① From *chūdan-no-kamae*, both players push forward and establish an *issoku ittō no maai*.

② Swing up your *shinai* swiftly until you can see the strike target (in this case, the *kote*) between your raised arms.

③ As you throw your left foot back, take a large stride with your right foot and swiftly swing down the raised *shinai*.

④ As your right foot hits the floor, hold the *shinai* in *tenouchi* and strike your opponent's *kote* accurately with the *monouchi*.

✳ **Strike with your *shinai* parallel to your opponent's *shinai*.**

Tobikomi-dō ④

＊ **Keep your left fist in line with the center of your body. Keep your upper body straight. Swiftly pull back your left foot and straighten your back.**

3. Tobikomi-dō

① From *chūdan-no-kamae*, both partners push forward and establish an *issoku ittō no maai*.

② At the precise moment your opponent swings up his *shinai* in a large movement, advance your right foot and swiftly swing up your *shinai* in a centered straight line.

③ When the *shinai* is above your head, twist your wrist to the left and swing down the *shinai* at an angle, with the cutting edge in the correct position.

④ Step forward with your right foot and strike your opponent's right *dō*. Extend your right arm and use both wrists to execute your strike.

Tobikomi-dō ①②③

Hikibana-kote ①

* The relationship between steps ② and ③ is important. This is a difficult *waza* for your opponent, since when you move forward into *issoku ittō no maai* you will force him to become agitated, lose his composure, and make his *kensen* rise.

4. Hikibana-kote

① Both players assume *chūdan-no-kamae*, at a distance where the *kensens* are not touching.

② Move in a straight centered line toward your opponent, with your right foot leading in *okuri-ashi*, and establish an *issoku ittō no maai*.

③ Your opponent will feel threatened, his mind will waver, his composure will give way, and his *kensen* will rise.

④ At the moment your right foot hits the floor, hold the *shinai* in *tenouchi* and swiftly strike your opponent's right *kote*.

Hikibana-kote ②③④

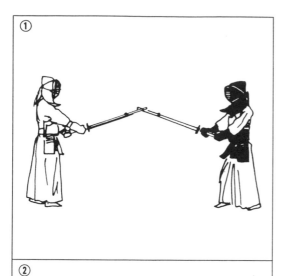

5. *Katsugi-kote*

① Both players assume *chūdan-no-kamae* and push forward to establish an *issoku ittō no maai*.

② Stepping forward with your right foot, move as if to check your opponent's *shinai* from the right.

③ After watching for the right moment, put your *shinai* on your right shoulder; this will surprise and confuse your opponent.

④ Your opponent will lose his poise and his *kensen* will rise. At this moment swing down your *shinai* (parallel to your opponent's *shinai*) and strike right *kote*.

∗ **Overcome your opponent with self-confidence.**

∗ **Repeated use of this *waza* will lose its surprise effect.**

From top left, *kote-men* ①②③④⑤

6. *Kote-men*

① From *chūdan-no-kamae*, both players push forward and establish an *issoku ittō no maai*.

② Stepping forward with your right foot, swing up your *shinai* until you can see your opponent's *kote* between your raised arms.

③ As you throw your left foot back, step forward with your right foot and hold your *shinai* in *tenouchi* as you strike right *kote* accurately with the cutting edge.

④ Without hesitating, draw your left foot toward your right foot and swing up the *shinai* until you can see your opponent's *men* between your raised arms.

⑤ Advance with your right foot, swing down your *shinai*, and as your right foot hits the floor, hold your *shinai* in *tenouchi* and strike *shōmen* accurately with the *monouchi*.

✳ With *renzoku-waza* the drawing forward of your left foot toward your right foot is crucial.

✳ The *tenouchi* should be tightened and relaxed with each strike. You must utilize the *tenouchi* skillfully.

From top left, *kote-dō* ①②③④⑤⑥

7. *Kote-dō*

① From *chūdan-no-kamae*, both players push forward to establish an *issoku ittō no maai.*

② Swing up your *shinai* until you can see your opponent's *kote* between your raised arms.

③ Move your right foot forward quickly, hold your *shinai* in *tenouchi,* and strike right *kote* sharply.

④ At the precise moment your opponent draws back his left foot and swings up his *shinai,* swing up your *shinai* until you can see his *dō* between your raised arms.

⑤⑥ Next, twist your wrist to the left above your head and swing down the cutting edge accurately to the right; as you step diagonally to the right with your right foot, strike right *dō.*

From top left, *men-dō* ①②③④⑤

* When you attack *kote*, it causes your opponent to raise his hand in an attempt to evade the strike.

* Drawing your left foot forward to your right is very important.

8. *Men-dō*

① From *chūdan-no-kamae*, both players push forward to establish an *issoku ittō no maai*.

② Swing up your *shinai* until you can see your opponent's *men* between your raised arms.

③ Step forward quickly with your right foot, hold the *shinai* in *tenouchi* and strike *shōmen* sharply.

④ At the precise moment your opponent draws back his left foot and swings up his *shinai*, swing up your *shinai* until you can see his *dō* between your raised arms.

⑤ Next, twist your wrist to the left above your head, and swing down the cutting edge accurately to the right; as you step diagonally to the right with your right foot, strike right *dō*.

* Effective against opponents who raise their hands when attacked at *men*.

From top left, *harai-age-men* (*omote*) ①②③④⑤

✻ **Maintain a rhythm between the start of sweeping your opponent's *shinai* and the execution of a strike on *men*.**

9. *Harai-age-men* (*omote*)

① From *chūdan-no-kamae*, move forward quickly from your right foot, and lower the *kensen* to the right as if drawing an arc.

② At the moment the *kensen* is lowered, sweep your opponent's *shinai* sharply up to the left with the left side of your *shinai*.

③ Bring the *shinai* directly above your opponent's *men*.

④ Sweeping upward, begin to move your right foot forward.

⑤ As your right foot hits the floor, hold your *shinai* in *tenouchi* and strike *shōmen* accurately with the *monouchi*.

10. *Harai-age-men* (*ura*)

① From *chūdan-no-kamae*, both players push forward and establish *tōma*, at an interval in which the *kensen*s touch slightly.

② Move forward quickly with your right foot and lower the *kensen* to the left as if drawing an arc, bringing it underneath your opponent's *shinai*.

From top left, *harai-age-men* (*ura*) ①②③④⑤⑥

③ At the moment the *kensen* is lowered, sweep your opponent's *shinai* with the right side of your *shinai* sharply up and to the right.

④ Bring the *kensen* of your own *shinai* directly above your opponent's *men*.

⑤ As you sweep upward, step forward with your right foot.

⑥ As your right foot hits the floor, hold the *shinai* in *tenouchi* and strike *men* accurately with the *monouchi*.

＊ *Harai-waza* is used when there is no *suki* in your opponent's *kamae*. By sweeping your opponent's *shinai* forward, backward, upward or downward, your opponent's *kamae* is broken, and you can initiate a strike.

＊ You should perform *keiko* adjusting the sweeping action appropriate to your opponent's *kamae*.

From top left, *harai-kote* (*ura*) ①②③④⑤

11. *Harai-kote* (ura)

① From *chūdan-no-kamae*, both players push forward and establish an *issoku ittō no maai*.

② Move forward quickly with your right foot and lower the *kensen* to the left as if drawing an arc, bringing it underneath your opponent's *shinai*.

③ At the moment the *kensen* is lowered, sweep your opponent's *shinai* with the right side of your *shinai* sharply up and to the right.

④ Bring the *kensen* of your own *shinai* to the mid-point of your opponent's right *kote*.

⑤ As the right foot hits the floor, swing down your own *shinai*, hold the *shinai* in *tenouchi*, and strike right *kote*.

❋ **This *waza* is particularly fast between the sweeping action and the execution of the strike.**

12. *Harai-otoshi-men* (omote)

① From *chūdan-no-kamae*, both players push forward and establish an *issoku ittō no maai*.

② Move forward swiftly with your right foot and raise the *kensen* diagonally to the right.

③④ At the moment the *kensen* is raised, sweep your opponent's *shinai* sharply with the left side of your *shinai* down and to the left.

From top left, *harai-otoshi-men* (*omote*)
①②③④⑤⑥

⑤ Drawing forward your left foot toward your right foot, swing up the *shinai* in a large movement.

⑥ As your right foot hits the floor, hold the *shinai* in *tenouchi* and strike *shōmen* accurately with the *monouchi*.

✳ **At the moment you sweep your opponent's *shinai*, hold your *shinai* in *tenouchi* as if you were about to execute a strike, and perform the sweeping action sharply.**

13. *Debana-men*

① From *chūdan-no-kamae*, both players push forward and establish an *issoku ittō no maai*.

② At the moment your opponent attempts to execute a strike, immediately swing up your *shinai*.

③ As you throw your left foot back, step forward with your right foot and swing down your *shinai*.

④ As your right foot hits the floor, hold the *shinai* in *tenouchi* and strike *shōmen* accurately with the *monouchi*.

- Execute the strike as soon as your opponent begins to move without even a split-second delay.

＊ It is important to maintain a posture of readiness at all times.

＊ Imagine that you are executing the strike from right on top of your opponent.

＊ *Debana* represents a *datotsu no kōki* (a good opportunity to execute a strike or thrust). Watch your opponent's movements well, and develop the eye and sense to perceive *debana*.

From top left, *debana-men* ①②③④

From top left, *debana-kote* ①②③④

14. *Debana-kote*

① From *chūdan-no-kamae*, both players push forward and establish an *issoku ittō no maai*.

② At the moment your opponent looks as if he is about to step forward with his right foot in an attempt to execute a strike, immediately swing up your *shinai*.

③④ When your opponent's *kensen* rises in an attempt to swing up his *shinai* as he steps forward with his right foot, hold your *shinai* in *tenouchi* and strike right *kote*.

✳ **The timing of *debana-kote* is the moment your opponent swings his *shinai* up in an attempt to strike.**

✳ **It is important for your *kensen* to travel through a straight line, as if you were attacking right through the center of your opponent.**

(2) Ōji-Waza

15. Men-nuki-dō

① From *chūdan-no-kamae*, both players push forward and establish an *issoku ittō no maai*.

② Your opponent swings up his *shinai* in order to strike your *men*. (You remain motionless.)

③ When your opponent begins to swing his *shinai* down, immediately step forward diagonally with your right foot and swing your *shinai* up.

④⑤ Twisting both wrists to the left, swing your *shinai* down from left to right.

⑥ Remain close to your opponent as you pass in the evasion, and as your right foot hits the floor hold the *shinai* in *tenouchi* and strike right *dō*.

✳ **Fast *ashi-sabaki* is necessary!**

From top left, *men-nuki-dō* ①②③④⑤⑥

76   Chapter 3

From top left, *kote-nuki-men* ①②③④⑤⑥

16. *Kote-nuki-men*

① From *chūdan-no-kamae*, both players push forward and establish an *issoku ittō no maai*.

② Your opponent swings his *shinai* up in order to strike your *kote*. (You remain motionless.)

③ As your opponent begins to swing his *shinai* down in an attempt to strike *kote*, draw your left foot back and swing your *shinai* up quickly in a straight line, avoiding his strike.

④ If you do not evade his strike positively and deliberately you will receive a strike on the *kote*, so take care to use a large movement so that both fists come right up above your head, as shown in the illustration.

⑤⑥ After successful evasion of the strike, immediately step forward with your right foot, and as it hits the floor hold the *shinai* in *tenouchi* and strike *men* accurately with the *monouchi*.

✳ Use the *chōyaku suburi* method.

✳ There are different types of *kote-nuki*: 1) remaining in *chūdan*, evading from the rear; 2) evading from below; 3) evading from above, etc.

From top left, *kote-nuki-kote* ① ② ③ ④ ⑤ ⑥

17. *Kote-nuki-kote*

① From *chūdan-no-kamae*, both players push forward and establish an *issoku ittō no maai*.

② Your opponent swings his *shinai* up in order to strike your *kote*. (You remain motionless.)

③ When your opponent begins to swing his *shinai* down, step back with your left foot and immediately draw your right foot toward the left, lower your *shinai*, and evade the strike.

④⑤ As you evade the *kote* strike, swing your *shinai* swiftly up.

⑥ As your right foot hits the floor, hold the *shinai* in *tenouchi* and execute a strike to right *kote*.

From top left, *men-suriage-men* (*omote*)
①②③④⑤⑥

18. *Men-suriage-men* (*omote*)

① From *chūdan-no-kamae*, both players push forward and establish an *issoku ittō no maai*.

② Your opponent swings his *shinai* up in order to strike your *men*. (You remain motionless.)

③ When your opponent begins to swing his *shinai* down, step forward diagonally with your right foot and slide the left side of your *shinai* up sharply, as if drawing an arc, parrying your opponent's *shinai* in a rising-slide motion (*suriage*).

④ Swing your *shinai* up during *suriage*.

⑤⑥ Bringing your left foot forward toward the right, execute a strike to *shōmen*.

✳ **Master the difficult timing of this complicated technique.**

✳ **Watch the position of your feet.**

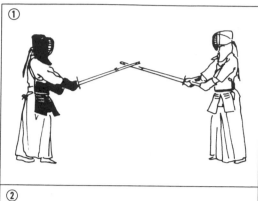

From top left, *men-suriage-men* (ura) ①②③④⑤⑥

19. *Men-suriage-men* (ura)

① From *chūdan-no-kamae*, both players push forward and establish an *issoku ittō no maai*.

② Your opponent swings up his *shinai* in order to strike *men*. (You remain motionless.)

③ When your opponent begins to swing his *shinai* down, step back diagonally with your left foot and slide the right side of your *shinai* up sharply, as if drawing an arc, parrying your opponent's *shinai* in a rising-slide motion (*suriage*).

④ Swing your *shinai* up during *suriage*.

⑤⑥ Drawing your right foot back, execute a strike to *shōmen*.

＊ Use *ashi-sabaki* during *suriage*.

＊ When your opponent moves vigorously forward, execute your strike as you step back diagonally.

20. *Kote-suriage-men* (ura)

① From *chūdan-no-kamae*, both players push forward and establish an *issoku ittō no maai*.

② Your opponent swings his *shinai* up in order to strike *kote*. (You remain motionless.)

③④ When your opponent begins to swing his *shinai* down, slide the right side of your *shinai* up sharply, as if drawing an arc, parrying your opponent's *shinai* in a rising-slide motion (*suriage*).

⑤ Swing your *shinai* up during *suriage*.

⑥ Step forward with your right foot, and as it hits the floor hold the *shinai* in *tenouchi* and execute a strike accurately to *shōmen* with the *monouchi*.

✳ Remember that *suriage* is not the aim of this exercise, but rather the means of executing a strike to *men*.

From top left, *kote-suriage-men* (ura) ①②③④⑤⑥

From top left, *kote-suriage-kote* ①②③④⑤⑥

21. *Kote-suriage-kote*

① From *chūdan-no-kamae*, both players push forward and establish an *issoku ittō no maai*.

② Your opponent swings his *shinai* up in order to strike your *kote*. (You remain motionless.)

③ When your opponent begins to swing his *shinai* down, step back diagonally with your left foot and extend both arms forward as if drawing an arc with the right side of your *shinai*; as you swing the *shinai* up, parry your opponent's *shinai* sharply in a rising-slide motion (*suriage*).

④⑤ Swinging your *shinai* up, bring the *kensen* directly above your opponent's right *kote*.

⑥ Drawing back your right foot, face your opponent squarely, hold the *shinai* in *tenouchi*, and execute a strike sharply to right *kote*.

❋ **Since this is a *kowaza* (*waza* using a small movement), it will only be effective if the *tenouchi* is correct. It is essential to master the skill of *tenouchi*.**

22. *Dō-uchiotoshi-men*

① From *chūdan-no-kamae*, both players push forward and establish an *issoku ittō no maai*.

② Your opponent swings his *shinai* up in

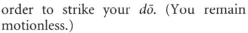

order to strike your *dō*. (You remain motionless.)

③ When your opponent swings his *shinai* down, step back diagonally with your left foot, swinging your *shinai* up.

④ Drawing your right foot back, hold the *shinai* in *tenouchi* and strike your opponent's *shinai* sharply down to the right on the *tsubamoto* (sword guard).

⑤ Stepping forward with your right foot, swing the *shinai* up over your head.

⑥ As your right foot hits the floor, hold the *shinai* in *tenouchi* and execute a strike accurately to *men* with the *monouchi*.

✳ **If your opponent moves vigorously forward, then you can execute the strike as you move back.**

From top left, *dō-uchiotoshi-men* ①②③④⑤⑥

23. *Kote-uchiotoshi-men*

① From *chūdan-no-kamae*, both players push forward and establish an *issoku ittō no maai*.

② Your opponent swings his *shinai* up in order to strike your *kote*. (You remain motionless.)

③ When your opponent swings his *shinai* down, step diagonally back with your left foot and swing your *shinai* up.

④ Drawing your right foot back, hold the *shinai* in *tenouchi* and strike your opponent's *shinai* sharply down to the right on the *tsubamoto*.

⑤ Step forward with your right foot and swing the *shinai* up over your head.

⑥ As your right foot hits the floor, hold the *shinai* in *tenouchi* and execute a strike accurately to *men* with the *monouchi*.

∗ **When striking the *kote* downward, use a small, sharp movement.**

From top left, *kote-uchiotoshi-men* ①②③④⑤⑥

* If unable to strike downward, first strike *kote* at the same time as your opponent, then strike *men*.

24. *Men-kaeshi-dō*

① From *chūdan-no-kamae*, both partners push forward and establish an *issoku ittō no maai*.

② Your opponent swings his *shinai* upward, in order to strike your *men*. (You remain motionless.)

③④ When your opponent begins to swing his *shinai* down, step diagonally forward with your right foot and counter your opponent's *men* strike with the left side of your *shinai*.

⑤ Counter your opponent's strike as though you were drawing his *shinai* toward you, and then step forward with your right foot, hold the *shinai* in *tenouchi*, and execute a strike to right *dō*.

* When countering your opponent's strike, do so as though you were drawing his *shinai* toward you.

* At the precise moment you counter your opponent's strike, flip your wrists over and strike swiftly.

From top left, *men-kaeshi-dō* ①②③④⑤

From top left, *kote-kaeshi-men* ①②③④⑤⑥

25. *Kote-kaeshi-men*

① From *chūdan-no-kamae*, both players push forward and establish an *issoku ittō no maai*.

② Your opponent swings his *shinai* up in order to strike your *kote*. (You remain motionless.)

③ When your opponent begins to swing his *shinai* down, step diagonally back with your left foot and counter your opponent's *shinai* with the left side of your own, as if drawing a semi-circle with the *kensen* downward to the right.

④⑤ Using the force of his strike, swing the *shinai* up over the head.

⑥ Step forward with your right foot, and as it hits the floor hold your *shinai* in *tenouchi* and execute a strike accurately to *men* with the *monouchi*.

∗ Use the force of your opponent and his *shinai* when carrying out *kaeshi-waza*.

∗ Your wrists should remain flexible.

26. *Kote-kaeshi-kote*

① From *chūdan-no-kamae*, both players push forward and establish an *issoku ittō no maai*.

② Your opponent swings his *shinai* up in order to strike your *kote*. (You remain motionless.)

③ When your opponent begins to swing his *shinai* down, step diagonally back with your left foot and counter his *shinai* with the left side of your own, as if drawing a semi-circle down to the right with the *kensen*.

④⑤ Keeping your wrists flexible, use the force of his strike to swing the *kensen* to the right (in the opposite direction from the one in which you countered his *shinai*) and swing your *shinai* up.

⑥ Drawing your right foot back, face your opponent squarely, hold the *shinai* in *tenouchi*, and execute a strike to right *kote*.

✳ **Keep your wrists flexible.**

From top left, *kote-kaeshi-kote* ①②③④⑤⑥

(3) *Tsubazeriai* and *Waza* from *Tsubazeriai*

Tsubazeriai describes the situation in which you and your opponent hold your *shinai*s upright, gripping them at the *tsuba-moto* (sword-guard), and stand in close physical contact with each other, assuming a *kamae* which enables you to respond at any moment to any change in your opponent.

In this situation, the *shinai*s intersect closely at the level of the *tsubamoto*. Since you are in very close contact with your opponent, the position is one of high tension. From such a position, you can break your opponent's poise and strike as you move back, as well as move forward and strike when your opponent is striking as he moves back.

27. *Hiki-men* from *Tsubazeriai*

① In the *tsubazeriai* position, watch for an opportunity to act. Maintain a physical stance which enables you to move forward at any time your opponent moves back.

② At the precise moment your opponent's hand moves back, shift back your center of mass and begin to step back as you swing up your *shinai*.

③ Step back with your left foot, then the right, quickly swing the *shinai* down, and strike *shōmen*.

④ At the execution of the *shōmen* strike, raise the *kensen* as you move back and quickly establish a *maai* which will enable you to avoid your opponent's attack.

⑤ Establish a *maai* of at least *issoku ittō*, assume *chūdan-no-kamae*, and maintain *zanshin*. (This applies also to 28 and 29 below.)

Above and right, *hiki-men* from *tsubazeriai*
①②③④⑤

For *hiki-waza*, strike forcefully

28. *Hiki-dō* from *Tsubazeriai*

① In the *tsubazeriai* position, watch for an opportunity to act. Maintain a physical stance which enables you to move forward at any time your opponent moves back.

② At the precise moment your opponent's hand is raised, or pushed up as a reaction to pressure exerted from the upper right to the lower left, or when you push your opponent's hand up, step back on your left foot and quickly swing up your *shinai*.

③④ Taking a large step back with your left foot, flipping both wrists to the left, swing your *shinai* down. Then, draw your left foot back even further to establish appropriate *maai*, hold the *shinai* in *tenouchi*, and execute a strike to right *dō* correctly with the cutting edge of the *monouchi*.

✳ **Strike correctly with the cutting edge.**

Hiki-dō from *tsubazeriai* ①②③④

From top left, *hiki-kote* from *tsubazeriai*
①②③④⑤

29. *Hiki-kote* from *Tsubazeriai*

① In the *tsubazeriai* position, watch for an opportunity to act. Maintain a physical stance which enables you to move forward at any time your opponent moves back.

②③ At the precise moment your opponent's hand is raised, or your opponent pushes back against the pressure exerted from the right to the left, quickly step back with your left foot and swing your *shinai* up.

④⑤ Drawing your right foot back toward the left, swing your *shinai* down and execute a sharp strike to right *kote*.

From top left, *suriage-men* (*omote*) against *hiki-men* from *tsubazeriai* ①②③④⑤

30. *Suriage-men* (*omote*) against *Hiki-men* from *Tsubazeriai*

① In the *tsubazeriai* position, watch for an opportunity to act. Maintain a physical stance which enables you to move forward at any time your opponent moves back.

② Your opponent swings his *shinai* up in order to strike *hiki-men*.

③④ At the precise moment he steps back and swings his *shinai* down in an attempt to strike *shōmen*, use the left side of your *shinai* to sharply parry his *shinai* up to the left in a rising-slide motion (*suriage*), as if drawing an arc.

⑤ Step forward with your right foot, and as it hits the floor hold the *shinai* in *tenouchi* and execute a strike to *shōmen* with the *monouchi*.

✳ As soon as your opponent strikes and begins to move back, do not hesitate in moving in to strike.

31. *Suriage-men* (*ura*) against *Hiki-men* from *Tsubazeriai*

① In the *tsubazeriai* position, watch for an opportunity to act. Maintain a physical stance which enables you to move forward at any time your opponent moves back.

② Your opponent swings his *shinai* up in order to strike *hiki-men*.

③④ At the precise moment he steps back and swings his *shinai* down in an attempt to strike *shōmen*, use the right side of your *shinai* to sharply parry your opponent's *shinai* up to the right in a rising-slide motion (*suriage*), as if drawing an arc.

⑤ Stepping forward with your right foot, immediately swing down the *shinai*.

⑥ As your right foot hits the floor, hold the *shinai* in *tenouchi* and execute a strike to *shōmen* with the *monouchi*.

From top left, *suriage-men* (*ura*) against *hiki-men* from *tsubazeriai* ①②③④⑤⑥

32. *Uchiotoshi-men* (*omote*) against *Hiki-men* from *Tsubazeriai*

① In the *tsubazeriai* position, watch for an opportunity to act. Maintain a physical stance which enables you to move forward at any time your opponent moves back.

② Your opponent swings his *shinai* up in order to strike *hiki-men*.

③ At the precise moment he steps back and swings his *shinai* down in an attempt to strike *shōmen*, step forward with your right foot and, using the left side of your *shinai*, begin to strike his *shinai* down to the left (*uchiotoshi*).

④ When the *uchiotoshi* technique is complete and your opponent's *shinai* has been knocked right down, quickly draw your left foot toward the right.

⑤ Step forward with your right foot and swing your *shinai* up.

⑥ As your right foot hits the floor, hold the *shinai* in *tenouchi* and execute a strike to *shōmen* with the *monouchi*.

From top left, *uchiotoshi-men* (*omote*) against *hiki-men* from *tsubazeriai* ①②③④⑤⑥

33. *Uchiotoshi-men* (*ura*) against *Hiki-men* from *Tsubazeriai*

① In the *tsubazeriai* position, watch for an opportunity to act. Maintain a physical stance which enables you to move forward at any time your opponent moves back.

② Your opponent swings his *shinai* up in order to strike *hiki-men*.

③④ At the precise moment he steps back and swings his *shinai* down in an attempt to strike *shōmen*, step forward with your right foot and use the right side of your *shinai* to sharply strike his *shinai* down to the right (*uchiotoshi*).

⑤⑥ Immediately draw your left foot forward and, taking a large step forward with your right foot, swing your *shinai* up. As your right foot hits the floor, hold your *shinai* in *tenouchi* and execute a strike to *shōmen* with the *monouchi*.

From top left, *uchiotoshi-men* (*ura*) against *hiki-men* from *tsubazeriai* ①②③④⑤⑥

34. *Uchiotoshi-men* against *Hiki-dō* from *Tsubazeriai*

① In the *tsubazeriai* position, watch for an opportunity to act. Maintain a physical stance which enables you to move forward at any time your opponent moves back.

② Your opponent swings his *shinai* up in order to strike *hiki-dō*.

③④ At the precise moment he steps back and swings his *shinai* down in an attempt to strike *dō*, step forward with your right foot and use the right side of your *shinai* to sharply strike his *shinai* down to the right (*uchiotoshi*).

⑤ Take a large step forward with your right foot, and swing the *shinai* up.

⑥ As your right foot hits the floor, hold the *shinai* in *tenouchi* and execute a strike to *shōmen* with the *monouchi*.

From top left, *uchiotoshi-men* against *hiki-dō* from *tsubazeriai* ①②③④⑤⑥

35. *Uchiotoshi-men* against *Hiki-kote* from *Tsubazeriai*

① In the *tsubazeriai* position, watch for an opportunity to act. Maintain a physical stance which enables you to move forward at any time your opponent moves back.

② Your opponent swings his *shinai* up in order to strike *hiki-kote*.

③④ At the precise moment he steps back and swings his *shinai* down in an attempt to strike *kote*, step forward with your right foot and use the right side of your *shinai* to sharply strike his *shinai* down to the right (*uchiotoshi*).

⑤ Take a large step forward with your right foot and swing up the *shinai*.

⑥ As your right foot hits the floor, hold the *shinai* in *tenouchi* and execute a strike to *shōmen* with the *monouchi*.

From top left, *uchiotoshi-men* against *hiki-kote* from *tsubazeriai* ①②③④⑤⑥

Chapter

NIHON KENDO KATA

Kata

Kirikaeshi Trains the Body, *Kata* Teaches Principles and Methods

Competitive participation is the ultimate aim of modern Kendo, which means that *shinai* Kendo is the main focus of *keiko*. *Nihon Kendo Kata* is practiced almost exclusively for passing examinations to advance to a higher grade, with the result that once the grading is over, the *Nihon Kendo Kata* is forgotten. For serious Kendoists, however, the study of *kata* is essential and learning *Nihon Kendo Kata* is the first step in this process. Through *kata*, you will learn the following:

1. Correct posture.
2. A clear eye—the ability to perceive an opponent's intentions.
3. Correct line of sword movement.
4. Speed of movement.
5. Accuracy of strikes and thrusts.
6. An understanding of the proper *maai* for strikes and thrusts.
7. A means of developing *kigurai* (noble bearing, pride, and dignity).
8. A means of developing *kiai* (projection of fighting spirit into a shout or cry, giving voice to your breath).
9. An understanding of when the opportunity is right to strike or thrust.
10. Various *waza*.

Regular practice of *kata* before *keiko* will improve the level of your *shinai keiko* as well as enrich its quality.

Nihon Kendo Kata Rules

1. The *uchidachi* has the role of teacher, the *shidachi* the role of student.
2. The *uchidachi* moves first, the *shidachi* slightly later in response to this movement; the *uchidachi* therefore leads the *shidachi*.
3. From the first sitting bow right through to the last sitting bow there should be no relaxing of concentration.
4. When moving your feet, in principle move forward with the leading (right) foot, and backward with the rear (left) foot.
5. *Ashi-sabaki* should be silent, and care taken to ensure that your toes do not point upward.
6. The *shidachi* establishes a *maai* which enables his *monouchi* to reach the point where he is going to deliver a strike or thrust.
7. The call is "*yah*" for *uchidachi* and "*toh*" for *shidachi*.
8. The *katana* (*habiki*—without a cutting edge) is used only on formal occasions. For everyday *keiko*, the *bokken* (wooden sword) is used.

9. In principle, the *uchidachi* and *shidachi* focus on each other's eyes, without wavering (*metsuke*).

10. *Zanshin* should be asserted with strong *kigurai*.

Ipponme—The First Long Sword *Kata*

Jōdan-no-kamae

1. Two-hand Left *Jōdan* (*Uchidachi*)

From *chūdan-no-kamae*, step forward with your left foot and swing up the *bokken*. Your left fist should be in a position approximately over your left foot. With the *bokken* at an angle of 30–45 degrees, assume a *kamae* which enables you to see your opponent's whole body from below your left fist, with the feeling that you are going to overpower him. Raise the *kensen* to point back to the right without loosening the grip of your left hand. Step forward on your left foot, point the end of your right foot slightly out, and raise your heel slightly.

2. Two-hand Right *Jōdan* (*Shidachi*)

From *chūdan-no-kamae*, swing up the *bokken*. Both fists and the *kensen* should be in a centered straight line. With the *bokken* at an angle of 30–45 degrees, assume a *kamae* which enables you to see your opponent's body from below your left fist, with the feeling that you are going to overpower him. The *kensen* should be pointing back and up.

- *Jōdan* is called the *kamae* of fire—*hi-no-kamae*—and is a *kamae* where a strong, attacking spirit is plainly shown.
- The disadvantage of *jōdan* is that it opens up the *tsuki*, *dō*, and *kote*, and is therefore a *kata* full of *suki* (unguarded points, openings for attacks).
- When assuming a *jōdan-no-kamae*, it is important to attack with a strong *kigurai*, and with the feeling of "Come and strike me wherever you like!"

Ipponme

Shidachi

① Assume a two-hand right *jōdan-no-kamae* and from your right foot take three steps forward, establishing the correct *maai*.

②③ Take one step back with your left foot and simultaneously evade the *bokken* of the *uchidachi* by drawing your hands back and upward in *nuki-waza*.

Make sure that the *kensen* does not fall to a point below fist level.

④ Step forward with your right foot and deliver a *shōmen* cut.

⑤ With a strong *kigurai*, bring the *kensen* down to focus on the center of the *uchidachi's* face, between his eyes.

⑥ Step forward with your left foot, assume two-hand left *jōdan*, swing the *bokken* up over your head, and assert *zanshin*. It is important to maintain good *zanshin* with a strong *kigurai*.

⑦ As *uchidachi* begins to return to *chūdan* from *gedan*, draw back your left foot and from a two-hand left *jōdan* slowly resume *chūdan-no-kamae*.

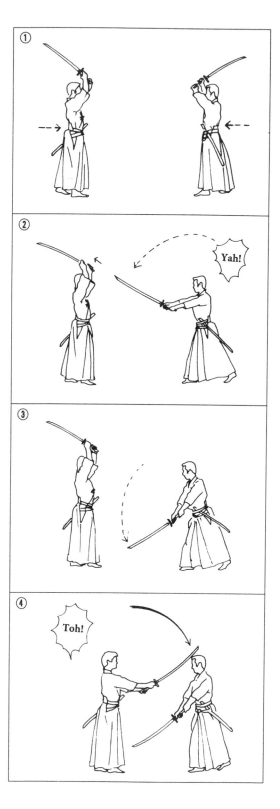

Uchidachi

① Assume a two-hand left *jōdan-no-kamae* and take three steps forward with your left foot, establishing the correct *maai*.

②③④ Watch for an opportunity to act, step forward with your right foot and execute a *shōmen* cut with an indomitable fighting spirit (*kigamae*). The cut should finish in a position slightly lower than the *shidachi's* knees.

⑤ With the *kensen* in *gedan*, take one step back with your left foot.

⑥ Take another step back.

⑦ Move your upper body into *chūdan-no-kamae*.

From top left, *ipponme* ①②③④⑤⑥⑦

Shidachi

① From *chūdan-no-kamae*, take three steps forward from your right foot, establishing the correct *maai*.

② Step diagonally back with your left foot and simultaneously evade the *uchidachi*'s *bokken* by lowering your *bokken* in an arc-like movement in *nuki-waza*.

③ Swing the *bokken* over and above your head.

④ Stepping forward from your right foot, deliver a cut to right *kote*.

⑤ Assert *zanshin* with a strong *kigurai*, and from your right foot return to *chūdan-no-kamae*.

Uchidachi

① From *chūdan-no-kamae*, take three steps forward with your right foot, establishing the correct *maai*.

②③④ Watch for an opportunity to act, swing your *bokken* up and over your head in a large movement, take one step forward with your right foot, and execute a cut to right *kote*. The cut should finish in a position slightly lower than the *shidachi*'s right *kote*.

⑤ Once the *shidachi* has completed his *zanshin*, assume *chūdan-no-kamae*. You should return to *chūdan* from below the *shidachi*'s sword.

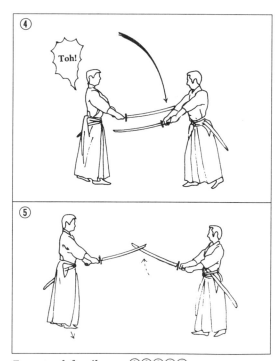

From top left, *nihonme* ①②③④⑤

Sanbonme—The 3rd Long Sword Form

Gedan-no-kamae

From *chūdan-no-kamae*, lower the *kensen* to a position slightly below your opponent's knees, as if you were going to attack his hands or feet.

- *Gedan-no-kamae* is effective as a defensive *kamae*, since your opponent will be afraid of receiving a thrust (*tsuki*) and at the same time is prevented by your *kensen* from easily executing a strike or thrust himself.

- Should your opponent attempt to make a strike or thrust, remain in *gedan-no-kamae* and thrust your *bokken* up aggressively.

Shidachi

① From *gedan-no-kamae*, take three steps forward with your right foot, establishing the correct *maai*.

② In a spirit of mutual combat (*kiarasoi***), move naturally to *chūdan-no-kamae*.

③ Taking a large step back with your left foot, deflect the *uchidachi's tsuki* (thrust) with the left *shinogi* (top edge) of the *bokken*, and turn it in your hands so that the cutting edge faces to your right—*ire zuki ni nayasu* (half-turned attitude of the body, so protecting your body by presenting a smaller area).

Kiarasoi—spirit of mutual combat. Overcoming an opponent with a vigorous spirit, pushing forward to break his guard.

Uchidachi

① From *gedan-no-kamae*, take three steps forward with your right foot, establishing the correct *maai*.

② In a spirit of mutual combat (*kiarasoi*), move naturally to *chūdan-no-kamae*.

③ Watch for an opportunity to act, point the *kensen* slightly to the right, and moving forward one step from your right foot deliver a thrust to the *shidachi's* solar plexus.

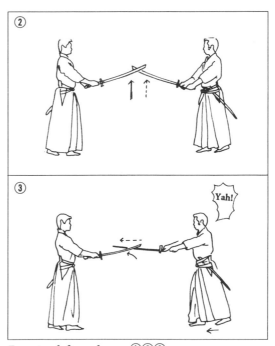

From top left, *sanbonme* ①②③

④ Against the weakening inward thrust of the *uchidachi*, do not cut with the edge of the blade but direct the end of the *bokken* straight down, take one step forward with your right foot, and counterthrust toward his chest.

⑤ Step forward with your left foot in the spirit of *tsuki*, and proceed in *kuraizume**. The *kensen* is at the level of the *uchidachi*'s chest.

⑥ Immediately take three steps forward from your right foot, and with a small quick step proceed in *kuraizume*. Gradually raise the *kensen* from chest level, so that it finally focuses on the center of the *uchidachi*'s face, and assert *zanshin*.

⑦ Step back with your left foot, then the right, and assume *chūdan-no-kamae*.

⑧ From your left foot, return to the original position of the *kensen*s meeting.

④ Step back with your right foot and at the same time bring your *kensen* under and around the *shidachi*'s *kensen*, slightly extend both arms, and assume a left *shizentai-no-kamae*. Direct the *kensen* to the *shidachi*'s throat. Push the *shidachi*'s sword to the right with the right *shinogi* of the *monouchi*.

⑤ Step back with your left foot, at the same time bringing the *kensen* under and around the *shidachi*'s sword, and assume a right *shizentai-no-kamae*. Push the *shidachi*'s sword to the left with the left *shinogi* of the *monouchi*.

⑥ Pressured by the *kigurai* of the *shidachi*, lower the *kensen* while stepping back three paces: left, right, left.

⑦ Once the *shidachi* has completed his *zanshin*, raise the *kensen* and assume *chūdan-no-kamae*.

⑧ From your right foot, return to the original position of the *kensen*s meeting.

*Kuraizume—the feeling of walking forward and pressing in on your opponent with a strong *kigurai*, as if, were your opponent to stop you, you would thrust your *bokken* through him.

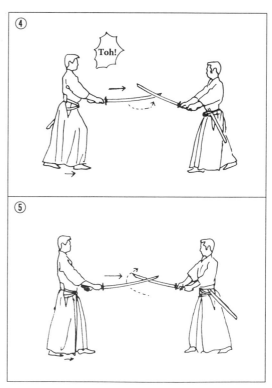

Sanbonme ④⑤

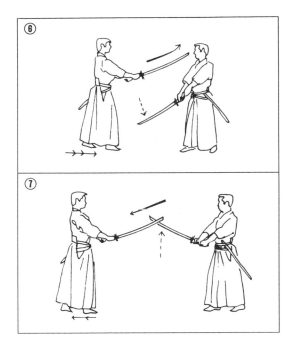

From top left, *sanbonme* ⑧⑦⑧

Yonhonme—The 4th Long Sword Form

Hassō-no-kamae (uchidachi)

From *chūdan-no-kamae*, assume a two-hand left *jōdan-no-kamae* and step forward with your left foot, the *tsuba* at mouth level—a distance of one fist away from your mouth—and point the cutting edge (*hasaki*) toward your opponent. Do not extend or contract your arms and keep your shoulders relaxed. Point your left foot forward and the end of your right foot slightly out, the heel slightly raised.

- *Hassō-no-kamae* is also called the *kamae* of wood—*moku-no-kamae*. Like a large tree rising high up into the sky, you assume a majestic and dignified stance to overcome your opponent.

- *Hassō-no-kamae* allows you to observe your opponent and change to an attacking posture in response to any forward movement from your opponent.

Wakigamae (shidachi)

From *chūdan-no-kamae*, step back with your right foot and bring the *kensen* down behind you, so that the sword is pointing down to the right. The important point is to assume a *kamae* which prevents the blade being seen by your opponent.

Your left foot should be pointing forward and the end of your right foot pointing slightly out, the heel slightly raised.

- *Wakigamae* is also called the *kamae* of metal—*kane-no-kamae*. Although in terms of form this does not seem to be an attacking *kamae*, you can in fact attack immediately from *wakigamae*.
- *Wakigamae* enables you to prevent your opponent knowing what weapon you hold. You can hold this *kamae* for a short or long time, depending on your opponent's movement.

Shidachi

① Step back with your right foot and assume *wakigamae*. Take three steps forward from your left foot, establishing the correct *maai*.

② At the same time, change from *wakigamae* to a two-hand left *jōdan-no-kamae*.

Uchidachi

① Step forward with your left foot and assume a *hassō-no-kamae*. Take three steps forward from your left foot, establishing the correct *maai*.

② Watch for an opportunity to act, and change from *hassō-no-kamae* to a two-hand left *jōdan-no-kamae*.

③ Both *shidachi* and *uchidachi* step forward with the right foot, and with a vigorous spirit attempt to deliver a simultaneous *shōmen* cut, so that the *shinogi* of the *bokken* lock together (*kirimusubi*).

④ After *aiuchi* (simultaneous cut or strike), they move their hands as if sharpening each other's blades, with strong *kigurai*, and assume *chūdan-no-kamae*.

If the *maai* is too close, the *uchidachi* should step back.

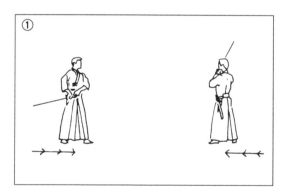

Yonhonme ① ②

⑤ Step forward to the left with your left foot, raise your left fist above your head, bring the cutting edge behind and swing it around in a large movement.

⑥ As you move your right foot back behind your left, swing the *bokken* down from above your head and deliver a *shōmen* cut to the *uchidachi*.

⑦ Asserting *zanshin* with a strong *kigurai*, return to the original position and assume *chūdan-no-kamae*.

⑤⑥ Watch for an opportunity to act, direct the cutting edge slightly to the right, then step forward from your right foot, at the same time pushing the *shidachi*'s sword down to the left, and make a thrust to his right lung.

⑦ From your left foot, return to the original position and assume *chūdan-no-kamae*.

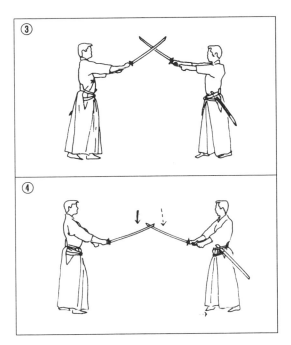

From top left, *yonhonme* ③④⑤⑥⑦

Shidachi

① Extend your *kensen* toward the *uchidachi's* left fist so that the cutting edge points down to the left and assume *chūdan-no-kamae.* Take three steps forward from your right foot and establish the correct *maai.*

② Take one step back with your left foot, and with the left *shinogi* deflect the *uchidachi's bokken* up by *suriage.*

③ Swing the *bokken* up over your head.

④ Step forward with your right foot and deliver a *shōmen* cut.

Uchidachi

① Step forward on your left foot and assume a two-hand left *jōdan-no-kamae.* Then take three steps forward from your left foot, establishing the correct *maai.*

② Watch for an opportunity to act, step forward with your right foot, and deliver a cut to the *shidachi's shōmen.*

③④ Lower the *bokken* to the right in a natural movement.

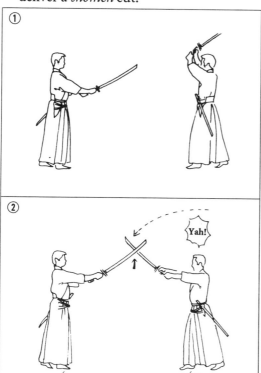

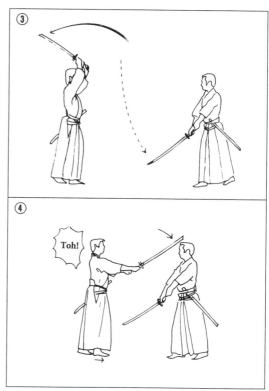

Gohonme ①②③④

⑤ Bring your *kensen* down from *shōmen*, directing it toward the center of the *uchidachi*'s face, between his eyes.

⑥ Step back with your right foot and assume a two-hand left *jōdan-no-kamae* with strong *zanshin*.

⑦ As the *uchidachi* begins to raise his *kensen*, step back with your left foot and assume *chūdan-no-kamae*. Then, from your right foot, advance three small steps and return to the original position.

⑤⑥ *Shidachi* asserts *zanshin*.

⑦ Once the *shidachi* has completed his *zanshin*, raise your *kensen* and assume *chūdan-no-kamae*. Then, from your left foot, take three small steps back and return to the original position.

From top left, *gohonme* ⑤⑥⑦

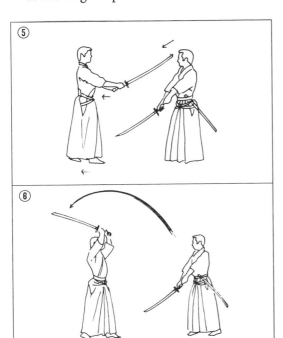

Ropponme—The 6th Long Sword Form

Shidachi

① In *gedan-no-kamae*, take three steps forward from your right foot, establishing the correct *maai*.

② Watch for an opportunity to act, and begin to raise your *kensen*, threatening with your rising *kamae* as though about to attack the center of the *uchidachi*'s fists.

③ From *chūdan-no-kamae*, immediately take one large step forward on your right foot to attack with strong *seme* (forward pressure), and direct the *kensen* at the *uchidachi*'s left fist.

④ Assume *chūdan-no-kamae*.

⑤⑥ Stepping around to the left with your left foot, deflect the *uchidachi*'s sword up by *suriage* with the right *shinogi*, in a small arc-like movement.

⑦ Step forward on the right foot and execute a cut to the *uchidachi*'s right *kote*.

⑧ Stepping forward on your left foot, use your *kensen* to exert forward pressure on the *uchidachi*.

⑨ Assume a two-hand left *jōdan-no-kamae* with strong *zanshin*.

⑩ As the *uchidachi* returns to his original position, return to your original position from the right foot and assume *chūdan-no-kamae*.

Uchidachi

① From *chūdan-no-kamae*, take three steps forward from your right foot, establishing the correct *maai*.

② Lower the *kensen* slightly, as though about to counter the *shidachi*'s attack.

③ The moment you attempt to meet the *shidachi*'s sword, do not allow yourself to be pushed back by his strength and pressure, but step back with your right foot and swing the sword up over your head in a two-hand left *jōdan-no-kamae*.

④ Immediately step back with your left foot and assume *chūdan-no-kamae*.

⑤⑥⑦ Watch for an opportunity to act, and strike the *shidachi*'s right *kote* with a small cut.

⑧⑨ Lower the *kensen* and turn the cutting edge to the right. Take a large step back to the left with your left foot.

⑩ Once the *shidachi* has completed his *zanshin*, return to your original position from the right foot and assume *chūdan-no-kamae*.

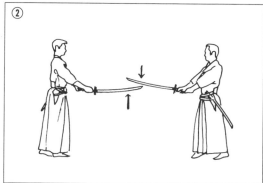

Ropponme ①②

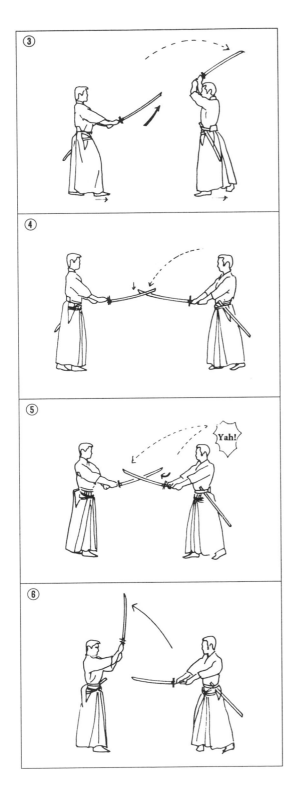

From top left, *ropponme* ③④⑤⑥⑦⑧⑨⑩

Shidachi

① From *chūdan-no-kamae*, take three steps forward from your right foot, establishing the correct *maai*.

② Step back from your left foot in accordance with the distance stepped forward by the *uchidachi*, and at the same time extend both hands with the spirit and vigor of *kiatari*—threatening a thrust to your opponent. Direct the cutting edge down slightly to the left, and with the left *shinogi* of the *monouchi* deflect the *uchidachi*'s *bokken*.

Uchidachi

① From *chūdan-no-kamae*, take three steps forward from your right foot, establishing the correct *maai*.

② Watch for an opportunity to act, take one light step forward on your right foot, and deliver a thrust into the *shidachi*'s chest. Turn the cutting edge down and slightly to the right.

③ Both *shidachi* and *uchidachi* establish *chūdan-no-kamae* with strong *kigurai*.

④ Step forward to the right with your right foot and at the same time raise the *bokken* up to the level of your left shoulder, holding a posture of *nuki-dō*.

④ Step forward on your left foot and swing the *bokken* up over your head.

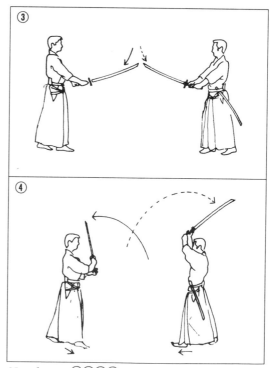

Nanahonme ①②③④

⑤ Step forward on your left foot and deliver a cut to the *uchidachi's* right *dō*.

⑥ Lower your right knee forward to the right and raise the left knee to face the *uchidachi*.

⑦ Turn the *bokken* over and assume *wakiga-mae*, making it clear you are still on guard by asserting *zanshin*.

⑤⑥ As you step forward on your right foot, try not to be self-conscious (*sutemi*) and deliver a full-blooded cut to the *shidachi's* *shōmen*.

⑦ Your *metsuke* moves away momentarily from the *shidachi*, but as soon as the cut has been executed, it returns to face the *shidachi*.

Nanahonme ⑤⑥⑦

⑧⑨ From *wakigamae*, swing the *bokken* in a large movement over your head. Then, pivoting on your right knee, change direction to face the left—you are now facing the *uchidachi*.

⑩ Step forward on your right foot, and with strength and vigor rise again to a standing position and assume *chūdan-no-kamae*.

⑧⑨ Raise your upper body, and as you swing the sword up over your head in a large movement pivot on your right foot and change direction to face left, then step back with your left foot and face the *shidachi*.

⑩ As if to draw the *shidachi* upward, step back from your left foot and assume *chūdan-no-kamae*.

⑪ Keeping the edges of the *bokken* together, both *shidachi* and *uchidachi* return from the left foot to their original positions.

Here the *bokken kata* end. Perform *sonkyo* and sheathe the *bokken* (*osame tō*).

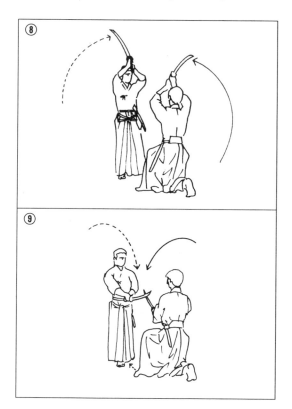

From top left, *nanahonme* ⑧⑨⑩⑪

Ipponme—The 1st Short Sword Form

Shidachi

① Assume *chūdan-hanmi-no-kamae* (position of *chūdan* with the *kodachi* positioned in response to the *uchidachi*'s *jōdan* or *gedan-no-kamae*), with the *kensen* slightly raised to focus on the center of the *uchidachi*'s face. Take three steps forward from your right foot and establish the correct *maai*. Concentrate on *irimi* (the action of stepping into your opponent's *maai*—fundamental short sword guard position).

② Stepping forward to the right with your right foot, raise your right hand over your head and with the left *shinogi* deflect the cut of the *uchidachi*, using the technique of *uke nagasu* (letting your opponent's attacking sword slide down along your blade). Turn the cutting edge to face the rear.

③ Step back with your left foot and at the same time deliver a cut to the *uchidachi*'s *shōmen*.

Uchidachi

① Assume a two-hand left *jōdan-no-kamae* and take three steps forward from your left foot, establishing the correct *maai*.

②③ Stepping forward with your right foot, deliver a downward cut to *shōmen*.

Kodachi ipponme ①②③

④ Take one step back from your left foot and assume a *jōdan-no-kamae*, asserting *zanshin* (with your right foot forward).

⑤ Assume *chūdan-no-kamae*.

④ *Shidachi* completes his *zanshin*.

⑤ Face the *shidachi* and assume *chūdan-no-kamae*. If the *maai* is too close, the *uchidachi* should move away.

⑥ From the left foot, both *shidachi* and *uchidachi* return to their original positions.

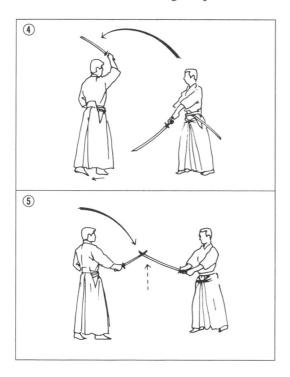

Kodachi ipponme ④⑤⑥

Kodachi nihonme—The 2nd Short Sword Form

Shidachi

① Assume a *chūdan-hanmi-no-kamae*, keeping the *kensen* in a slightly lower position (so that it comes to the *uchidachi*'s chest level). Take three steps forward from your right foot and establish the correct *maai*.

② Attack the *uchidachi*'s sword with the left *shinogi*, with a feeling of *irimi*.

③ Immediately returning to *chūdan-no-kamae*, move forward with the feeling of *irimi no seme* (entering by attacking your opponent's body).

Uchidachi

① Assume a *gedan-no-kamae* and take three steps forward from your right foot, establishing the correct *maai*.

② When defending, try to assume a *chūdan-no-kamae*.

③ Step back with your right foot and assume *wakigamae*.

④⑤ Change from *wakigamae* and swing the *bokken* over your head in a two-hand left *jōdan*, and as you step forward with your right foot deliver a full-blooded cut to the *shidachi*'s *shōmen*.

④ With your left foot step forward to the left and raise your right hand over your head and with the right *shinogi* deflect the *uchidachi*'s cut, using the *uke nagasu* technique. Turn the cutting edge to the rear.

⑤ Step back with your right foot, and at the same time face the *uchidachi* and deliver a *shōmen* cut.

⑥ With your left hand control the *uchidachi*'s right elbow from above, and at the same time bring the *kodachi* down to your right hip and assert *zanshin*. When you assert *zanshin*, turn the cutting edge to face away from you, and direct the *kensen* to the *uchidachi*'s throat.

⑦ From your right foot assume *chūdan-no-kamae* and return to your original position.

⑥ *Shidachi* completes his *zanshin*.

⑦ Assuming *chūdan* from your left foot, return to your original position.

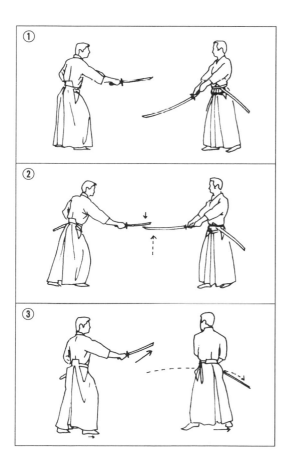

Kodachi nihonme ①②③④⑤⑥⑦

Shidachi

① Assume a *gedan-hanmi-no-kamae*, and move forward from your right foot, then the left.

②③ On the third step forward (right foot) as you attempt *irimi*, you will receive a *shōmen* attack from the *uchidachi*; at this point bring your *kodachi* straight up to deflect it with the left *shinogi* with the feeling of *suriage*, thus stopping his cut.

④ With a downward sliding motion (*suriotoshi*), throw the *uchidachi*'s sword to his right side.

Uchidachi

① In *chūdan-no-kamae*, move forward with your right foot, then the left.

②③④ On the third step (right foot), the *shidachi* will try to do *irimi*, and you should swing the *bokken* up over your head into a two-hand right *jōdan-no-kamae* and then bring it down to deliver a cut to the *shidachi*'s *shōmen*.

⑤ Move forward immediately with your left foot and execute a cut to the right *dō* of the *shidachi* with your sword which has been forced down in *suriotoshi*.

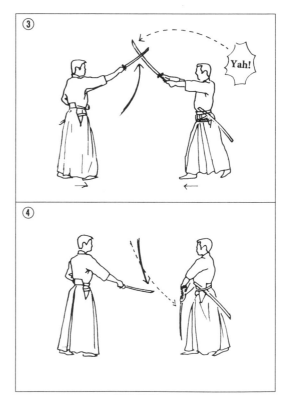

Kodachi sanbonme ①②③④

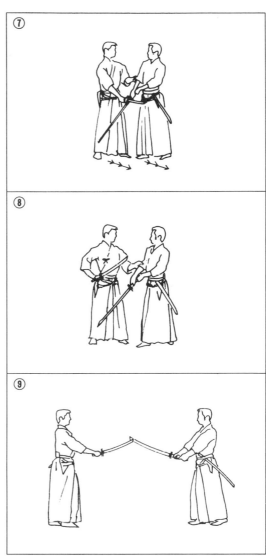

⑤ Step forward to the left on your left foot, and using your body in a turning motion away from the *uchidachi*, deflect his sword down with the left *shinogi*.

⑥ Slide your sword up to his *tsuba* with the left *shinogi* and press the base of your *tsuba* against his, and do *irimi*. With your left hand, grip his right arm slightly to the side of his elbow, restraining free movement of his arms. Lock his elbow with your left-hand grip.

⑦ Push forward three steps to the right with your left foot.

⑧⑨ Bring the *kodachi* to your right hip and assert *zanshin*, pointing the cutting edge down to the right and directing the *kensen* at the center of the *uchidachi*'s throat. After completing *zanshin*, from your left foot return to your original position.

Here the *kodachi kata* end. Perform *sonkyo* and sheathe the *kodachi* (*osame tō*).

Kodachi sanbonme ⑤⑥⑦⑧⑨

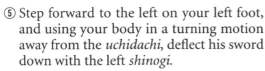

⑦ Take three steps back to the left from your right foot.

⑧⑨ Once the *shidachi* has completed his *zanshin*, from your right foot assume *chūdan-no-kamae* and return to your original position.

KEIKO (PRACTICE)

Suburi

Keiko: The Repetition of Basic Techniques

Kendo is fundamentally a form of physical exercise. The muscles used in Kendo must therefore be trained and built up through repeated practice of basic techniques. However, the repetition of simple techniques day after day requires considerable patience, so unless you enjoy it, or learn how to enjoy it, it will be impossible. Unfortunately, the muscles used in Kendo soon return to their original state if they are not used.

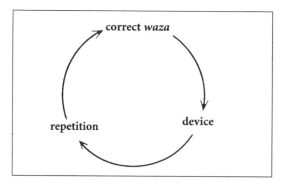

It may look easy when your instructor says "Hold the *shinai* like this, then strike the *men* like this." The body will only adapt naturally by devising correct techniques and repeating them in a single-minded fashion. In this way, speed, muscular strength, and skill will also be gradually cultivated. The diagram shows how the balance between the physical and mental aspects of Kendo changes during progress from beginner level to improver level. We can see how at beginner level the physical aspects predominate, and how, as the beginner makes progress, the mental aspects gradually assume importance.

Devices

Keiko must be taken very seriously, as if each session presented you with your last opportunity to get it right. This means saying to yourself, "This is my final chance for *keiko*

with this partner, so I must make sure I give it everything I have and leave no room for regret." For when it comes to individual *keiko* sessions there is a tendency to adopt a lazy attitude, to think that we can practice anytime. It is this kind of attitude which prevents real progress being made despite practicing every day. As long as you perform *keiko* seriously, concentrating fully on your opponent and using your whole body and nervous system, you can be assured of real improvement. Even when things do not go so well, you should not feel that you are just wasting your time. Both the way you attack and the way you strike are devices and not simply a matter of following a single pattern. If an attack from the left side (*omote*) fails, you must try attacking from the right side (*ura*). If this attack also fails, you should try once more from the left side. Devising different patterns for attacking and striking constitutes successful *keiko*.

Step-by-step progress to a future goal can be achieved through such an attitude toward *keiko*. More than that, each *keiko* practice should be approached as a valuable goal in itself. *Keiko* demands initiative and positive thinking precisely because it involves the repetition of simple, basic techniques.

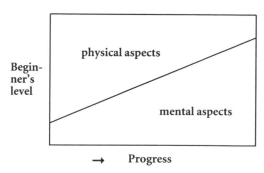

At the Beginner Level, Use *Waza* Freely

At the beginner level, when wishing to strike *men*, it is not enough simply to aim at the *men*; this would make *keiko* particularly monotonous. It is true, of course, that the words "Begin with *men*, end with *men*" are used in Kendo, emphasizing the importance of striking *men*. However, between the first and final *men* every single technique should be mastered. Thinking only of striking *men* would produce a dry and dull form of Kendo, completely lacking in intensity. In order to strike *men* you must observe the overall position of your opponent closely, with careful consideration of every possible reaction. This is what it means to attack, to push forward seeking to break your opponent's guard. All possible movements should be seen as a single flowing action that will enable you to devise a way to create an opening in *men*. You may, for example, consider a series of moves that will deflect your opponent's attention away from his *men*, making him think it is his *kote* that is in fact your target.

At the beginner level, it is also important to train yourself to use *waza* freely to strike *men*, *kote*, or *dō*. Regardless of whether you can actually use all these in *jigeiko* (free practice) or in matches, it is essential to teach your body techniques, since these kinds of *waza* sometimes emerge unconsciously in competition. In this way, *keiko* will take on increased depth and maturity, which in turn will enhance your confidence.

The Importance of "Big *Waza*" for Beginners

Strange as it may seem coming from a writer who has devoted so many pages to explaining technique, I would like to emphasize that you should not rely too heavily on *waza*. You should recognize that in Kendo spirit is always more important than *waza*, and it is the fundamentals of *keiko*—namely *kirikaeshi* (continuous strikes of right and left *men* alternately) and *kakarigeiko* (all-out attack practice)—which cultivate this spirit. Unfortunately, most people dislike them because they are the simplest and toughest parts of *keiko*. Nevertheless, it is vital to under-

stand the importance of these simple, tough, monotonous forms of *keiko*.

Instructors are advised not to overload students with detailed explanation of Kendo techniques, since this is liable to result in over-reliance on well-accomplished *waza* and can have the ultimate effect of inhibiting students' personal style. Beginners should perform *keiko* as far as possible with big *waza*—in other words, using a large movement for the upswing of the *shinai* and striking with conviction.

Receiving a Strike

If you find yourself on the receiving end of a strike it means that your opponent has exposed a lapse in your concentration, a weakness or *suki*. Respond to this first with humility and modesty, and then consider how not to be struck again in the same place. In this way, you can rectify your faults, improve your *keiko*, and make real progress.

Without appropriate humility it is quite difficult to advance in Kendo. Basically, it comes down to whether or not you are prepared to recognize your mistakes and try to make sure that they do not happen again. It is no good saying things like "That wasn't really a valid strike," or "It was only a feeble one." No matter how weak the strike may be, or how far off the mark—even if an attempt to strike *kote* (the forearm) lands on the fist—in order to ensure that you are not struck in the same place again, you must think about why it happened and how you could have fended it off. This leads to improvement.

Breaking the Barrier

Everything has a point of arrival. When climbing a mountain, that point is the summit. But once you reach the summit of one mountain you can go on to the next challenge, climbing an even higher one. For this endeavor, new factors and conditions need to be taken into consideration based on previous experience.

It is the same with Kendo. Take gradings, for example. When you try for 2nd Dan (grade), you need to take account of new factors based on what you have already learned. When you want to progress to 3rd Dan, you must fulfil the conditions of 2nd Dan as well as those of 3rd Dan. In order to make good progress, therefore, it is no good just continuing what you have been doing. Sometimes it is necessary to venture a step forward and take risks in order to break that barrier.

The Importance of Balanced Instruction

Too much emphasis placed on one particular aspect of instruction in the early stages often results in a failure to cultivate the innate talent of the beginner. Good Kendo can only come about through a resolute and genuine originality, but it would seem that this kind of Kendo has become almost impossible to attain. As mentioned at the beginning of this chapter, Kendo is practiced through devising correct *waza*, and then by continuous repetition of that *waza*. The use of such devices, however, has slackened in recent years.

Competition and with it the overemphasis on winning and losing may be the root of this problem. I do not object to the number of competitions in Japan every year and believe that individuals who wish to participate in competitions should be provided with the opportunity to do so. Children, however, are taught techniques for winning matches as soon as they take up Kendo, and this has made it difficult to practice relaxed and comprehensive Kendo. This has to do with the fact that many people nowadays take up Kendo in Japan in order to make a name for themselves. These people delude themselves into believing that they have mastered the true essence of Kendo merely because they have learned a few techniques useful for winning matches.

Beginners should concentrate, in the early stages at least, more on defeating themselves than their opponents.

The Sword Is the Person

Always remember that your style and behavior in Kendo will accurately reflect your personality. A quick-tempered player will produce quick-tempered Kendo. Likewise, a casual attitude will produce a casual style of Kendo. It goes without saying that you must have a large-scale personality to practice large-scale Kendo. One who performs particularly splendid Kendo will be the product of everything that he has lived and experienced. Your experiences and your life will inevitably affect your Kendo. You must cultivate both your mind and your body if you are to grasp the true essence of Kendo.

Enthusiasm and single-mindedness are the two most important qualities required for successful Kendo. In his *Academic Learning as Work*, Max Weber writes: "People who do not have the enthusiasm which enables them to feel no regret over the thought of spending a whole lifetime investigating one missing letter from an old moth-eaten manuscript are unsuited to academic learning." In Kendo, too, there are people who say "I perform *keiko* in order to strike just one perfect *men*." The idea behind this is fundamental to Kendo, and shows that if the purpose is not to achieve fame, neither is it to boast. A single-minded enthusiasm, with no expectation of material reward, is vital.

Kendo Is Infinite

When asked why you are learning Kendo,

how would you reply? Everyone will give a different response, according to age or other factors. But it is important to clarify your reasons for wanting to learn Kendo before you take it up. Kendo involves pitting yourself against an opponent in the *dōjō* and winning matches. This does not mean, however, that you should learn Kendo for the following reasons:

(1) to fight people

(2) for vanity

(3) to humiliate people

(4) to enhance reputation

(5) for financial gain

Always bear the above points in mind, and apply yourself single-mindedly to your *keiko*. Unfortunately, there are those who practice Kendo with enthusiasm but fail to heed these points, thinking only of immediate tangible results. Try not to be impatient to see improvements in your Kendo, and remember that the process is sometimes more important than the result. Too much concern with worldly goals and ambitions is likely to have an adverse effect on your Kendo. Further, it is a grave mistake to think that an understanding of technique will automatically enable you to grasp the essence; Kendo is infinite, so rather than focusing on winning or losing, think carefully about how to refine your skills.

Avoid Solitary Practice

Admiration for solitary practice in Kendo is misplaced. Growing up is of course a natural and, to some extent, a solitary process. If you are blessed with talent, you may advance to a certain level by following only your own desires, but that superior talent will eventually founder without reaching maturity. If the bud of your innate qualities is not constantly cultivated, it will not bloom prop-

erly. Thus the more talent you have, the more you need to practice *waza* with a good instructor and refine your spirit.

In both technical and spiritual terms, therefore, it is impossible to achieve first-class Kendo through self-study. Kendo past masters achieved their standing through learning from the strengths of their predecessors and assimilating these strengths into their own practice. To learn Kendo you must have a teacher and observe the way that teacher behaves in the *dōjō*, and the way he conducts his life.

Shugyō (Resident Student Training)

The system of *shugyō* is a traditional method of training no longer very common in the world of Kendo. Once permission has been granted, the student, or "disciple," moves in with the "master" and lives with him around the clock, day in, day out. This does not mean, however, that the disciple has more opportunity for *keiko*; in fact, most of his time is spent doing his master's household chores, such as cleaning and laundry. At the same time, however, the disciple is in a position to take a good look at the way his master instructs the students who come to him on a daily basis. The chance to observe closely in this way is the best training he could possibly have. Watching, listening to his master's careful instructions in training sessions, he naturally picks up various pointers for his own use. This is the fundamental concept of *shugyō*, the traditional method which advocates *waza* as something to be absorbed and appropriated by the individual. Things that are painstakingly taught are soon forgotten; in contrast, things acquired by devising one's own techniques through trial and error are learned through the body, and in this way are never forgotten.

So the resident disciple begins his *shugyō* by watching and studying. Through learning *waza* he gains first-hand experience of his master's character. Following the rhythm of his master's daily life, the disciple begins to assume the same Kendo posture, attitude, and philosophy. Before he knows it, his master's style of Kendo has become second nature. When we consider the extent to which the disciple is influenced in this way, there can be little doubt that the master's position is not an easy one.

Today, very few disciples reside with their master, a fact which may be connected to the relationship between teacher and student in modern city *dōjō*s. However, the instructor should never forget for a moment that he is being observed. Young people sow seeds which later put out shoots and ripen. The quality of the yield, however, depends on the seed that is sown, and thus the method of instruction is vital to the production of healthy fruit.

Following Superiors

In Kendo, you are always told to "follow your superiors" in *keiko*. A superior might be a master, teacher, or senior, someone who is stronger or more distinguished. Provided that he possesses the right qualities, a superior might even be younger than you. To "follow" means to respect a superior individual and seek guidance from that person with an open mind. If you adopt a frank and open-minded attitude, recognizing the value of your seniors and showing them due respect, you will eventually be able to rise to their standard. This is what is meant by the words "follow your superior." You must strive to identify with the ideas of someone better than yourself, to train yourself through direct contact with a genuine example of what you aspire to.

If You Run After Two Hares, You Will Catch Neither

There is a well-known proverb in Japan which is probably almost universally understood: "If you run after two hares, you will catch neither." In other words, if you are greedy and try to pursue two things at once, you will end up failing to achieve anything. The same applies to Kendo. To get past the first stage of Kendo when everything seems difficult, and then possibly to become really good at it, you need commitment. To achieve something big, you have to stake your whole life on it. It requires a large-scale personality, the mentality embodied in the saying "One road leads to ten thousand accomplishments."

Unfortunately, when you look around, you often think that the grass is greener on the other side. You are often unable to sit still and relax, and tend to follow what appears to be the right direction at that moment without really thinking the whole thing through. There is nothing so difficult as to pursue one thing without allowing

yourself to become distracted. In Kendo, even when you reach the age of seventy or eighty you cannot rest on your laurels; there will still be room for progress, and so the need for *shugyō* will continue.

The most important thing is to create a reserve within yourself that will never dry up. In other words, you should take care to ensure that your will to pursue Kendo does not get deflected, and strive constantly to focus wholeheartedly on it. Recently, there has been a trend toward adopting a wider approach, toward diversification rather than specialization. This is something you should be wary of, since the danger of such an attitude is that you will become a Jack-of-all-trades. Remember, "If you run after two hares, you will catch neither."

Continuous, Firm Strikes during Ordinary *Keiko*

When it comes to matches, few people can display any more strength than they do during normal *keiko*. In fact, some people produce even less than their usual strength, owing to nervousness. Thus, it is important that you perform ordinary *keiko* properly, so that you will not become easily flustered in competition. This means constantly training to be the first to execute a valid strike, with no unnecessary or futile movements. It also means being always responsive to your opponent's movements. Your *keiko* should therefore be conducted at a high pitch of alertness.

Cleaning the Floor Is Part of *Keiko*

Taking responsibility for keeping the place where you do *shugyō* clean and tidy is important for several reasons. It serves as a form of exercise for the legs and back. It helps you get into the right frame of mind for the start of *keiko*. And, as *keiko* is performed without footwear, it is essential that the floor be free of anything which might injure the feet, such as splinters from *shinai*. Moreover, if bits of rubbish or dust are left lying on the floor these can easily blow around and get sucked in by people during *keiko*, which could be harmful. Cleaning the floor of the *dōjō*, therefore, is significant in many ways.

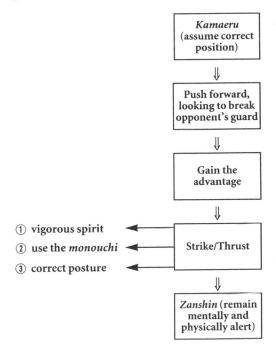

Practicing in a Large *Dōjō*

The way *keiko* is performed varies according to the size of the *dōjō*. In a small *dōjō* you can only do *nidan-waza* (two-step techniques) and *sandan-waza* (triple attack techniques) before colliding with the wall, and it is impossible to practice *renzoku-waza* (continuous attack techniques). One way of performing *ashi-sabaki* (footwork) *keiko* in a small *dōjō* is to do *suriashi* (gliding walk) for approximately twenty meters, leading with the right foot, taking care not to let the left foot protrude in front. The way to do this is to hold the *shinai* horizontally behind your body, hands hanging down by your sides freely and stretching your back so that the *shinai* is supported in the crook of each arm. The chest should be pushed out, while making sure the upper half of the body does not lean forward, and your eyes should face straight ahead.

Renzoku-waza can also be carried out with an imaginary opponent (using empty space). This is done by lining up together and making the motions of *renzoku-men* or *renzoku-kote*, with everyone executing the strike simultaneously. The strike is made by taking off from the left leg and making as long a jump forward as possible so that the right leg hits the floor firmly. Here, too, you should take care not to let the left leg protrude in front of the right. Also, when you become tired, your upswing naturally becomes smaller, so it is important to make sure that you swing the *shinai* right up over your head between each imaginary strike.

Musha Shugyō

The term *musha shugyō* is somewhat outdated, referring to the custom during the Edo period (1603–1868) of practitioners of martial arts going around the country performing *shugyō* in order to polish their skills. The same thing happens today, though we no longer refer to it by the same term. As far as Kendo is concerned, if you always perform *keiko* at the same *dōjō* with the same opponents, it is inevitable that your pitch of tension will eventually slacken and your *keiko* lose its freshness. When this happens, you can bring about an increased sense of tension and revitalize your *keiko* by going to another *dōjō*, or even to a completely different region. By going in the summer to somewhere with an even hotter climate, or in the winter to an even colder climate than your own, and by carrying out *shugyō* in these places, you are exposed to a new kind of hardship. Once you have overcome this, however, your confidence will increase enormously. By doing this again and again you will see an improvement in technical skills, as well as great spiritual benefits. Above all, it will make you more rich and rounded as a person. *Musha shugyō* is a very positive act, and we can gain a tremendous amount from it.

BASIC EXAMPLE OF PRACTICE PLAN

Kendo is a contest in which victory or defeat is decided in an instant. It is important, therefore, even in ordinary practice sessions to maintain an attitude of full concentration and vitality as you face your opponent. In addition, all movement and action between practice maneuvers should be brisk, for if you allow your movements to relax this will reflect clearly in your posture (*kamae*) and attitude when you face your opponent. You should therefore hold yourself in readiness at all times. This is particularly important when you consider that a strike with the *shinai* is followed by players colliding with each other in *taiatari*, a situation which could cause injury if you allowed yourself to relax. By maintaining total concentration at all times, the danger of injury occurring is negligible. Injury during practice is largely your own responsibility.

The following is a practice plan for a session of one hour and forty minutes, including some important points to note. The session should be carried out in the following order:

(1) Warm-up exercises

(2) Basic practice

(3) Arranged practice

(4) Combined practice

(5) Basic *waza, kirikaeshi*

(6) Regulated exercises

The time allocated to each section should be determined by the instructor and more experienced members of the club. This might, for example, be worked out at a regular weekly meeting during which the previous week could be reviewed and the plan for the following week discussed by everyone. Working as a team in this way is very important.

Time	Practice Content	Points to Note
10 min	Warm-up exercises	* Do not put on all the equipment at once. * Do not simply carry out as physical warm-up exercises, but as spiritual warm-up exercises too, as if gradually building up concentration.
10 min	*Ashi-sabaki, suburi* Advance and retreat, upward and downward *suburi* Advance and retreat *shōmen suburi* Advance and retreat left and right *men suburi* Forward and backward leaping *shōmen suburi*	For *ashi-sabaki* and *suburi*, face directly forward and perform as if an opponent is physically present.
5 min	Put on equipment Get into position for practice	Put on equipment while sitting in the *seiza* position.
15 min	Practice basic and applied *waza* *Kirikaeshi* Basic *waza* Applied *waza*	* Rather than practice many *waza* at beginner stage, carry out repeated practice of basic *waza*. * Gradually incorporate applied *waza* as progress is made, but concentrate on *shikake-waza*.
5 min	Check clothing and *shinai* Get into position for combined practice	* Check clothing while seated in the *seiza* position. * Movements while getting into position should be brisk.
10 min	Striking practice *Kakarigeiko*	* Execute each strike firmly. * The upward and downward sweep of the *shinai* should be large and swift.
5 min	Check clothing and *shinai* Get into position for combined practice	* Check clothing while seated in the *seiza* position. * Movements while getting into position should be brisk.
20 min	Combined practice	* The part of *motodachi* should be taken by the instructor and senior members. * Execute the first strike with total concentration. * Beginners who are not wearing the appropriate equipment should carry out *kirikaeshi* and *kakarigeiko* against the *motodachi*. * Carrying this out with opponents of the same level for about 5 minutes before finishing can be very stimulating, as you might have an opportunity to execute a successful strike.
10 min	Basic *waza* and *kirikaeshi*	Practice basic *waza* to correct *kamae* and the way of striking, which will have deteriorated during combined practice.
5 min	Remove *kote* and *men*	Line up in *seiza* and remove *kote* and *men*.
5 min	Regulated exercise	Finally, carry out deep breathing.

MEASUREMENT OF *FUMI-KOMI*

Maximum Force Generated by *Fumi-Komi-Ashi* with Right Foot on Contact with the Floor Surface during *Shōmen* and *Kote* Strike (*Shōmen-Uchi* and *Kote-Uchi*)

| | | Experienced | | | | Inexperienced | |
| | | Men | | Women | | | |
Direction		Maximum Force (kgw)	Magnification of Body Weight	Maximum Force (kgw)	Magnification of Body Weight	Maximum Force (kgw)	Magnification of Body Weight
Shōmen-Uchi	Right	73.1	1.10	50.4	0.83	21.0	0.29
	Left	39.1	0.60	29.0	0.49	23.7	0.37
	Forward	42.5	0.63	35.1	0.60	53.5	0.75
	Backward	85.0	1.25	70.0	1.23	17.0	0.24
	Perpendicular	884.0	13.1	548.0	9.36	408.0	5.4
Kote-Uchi	Right	68.0	0.99	44.2	0.75		
	Left	28.2	0.42	25.8	0.43		
	Forward	54.4	0.77	49.9	0.76		
	Backward	55.8	0.78	66.9	1.16		
	Perpendicular	769.5	11.4	523.4	9.04		

Fumi-komi-ashi refers to the movement of the right foot during a striking move. If the movement is not performed correctly, injury can easily occur, since a huge amount of force is generated at the instant the sole of the right foot comes into contact with the floor. This force is an important factor affecting the power of a strike, stability of posture, and recovery of balance after the strike has been executed.

Although many *dōjō*s are now equipped with improved floor spring, injury to the heel of the right foot when performing *fumi-komi-ashi* is still common, an indication that this movement is not being carried out correctly. On no account should padded support bandages be used to disguise a lack of skill in performing *fumi-komi-ashi*. Rather, begin by moving over a short distance, and extend the distance gradually as you become more familiar with the correct technique. It is important to perform *fumi-komi-ashi* at virtually the same time as you execute the strike.

Fumi-komi-ashi is, understandably perhaps, notorious in the world of Kendo. There are even tales of how at the moment of performing *fumi-komi-ashi* someone once actually slammed their foot right through the floor. So just how much force is generated?

Dr. Fuminori Nagiri, a scientific consultant for the All Japan Kendo Federation and a Professor of Tokyo University of Agriculture and Technology, used a special device to measure the force generated in three directions by the right foot at the moment of *fumi-komi-ashi*: forward and backward, left and right, and vertically downward. As shown in the table, a *shōmen* strike by a man generates an average force of 884.6 kgw in the vertically downward direction, 85 kgw in the backward direction, and 73.1 kgw in the right direction. In fact, some of those taking part in the experiment registered a force of over one tonne in the vertically downward direction. In the case of a *kote* strike, too, quite a large measure is evident—an average of 769.5 kgw in the vertically downward direction.

The figures recorded for women were naturally lower, owing to the comparative difference in physical strength. Nevertheless, the force was measured at an average of 548 kgw during a *shōmen* strike and 523.4 kgw during a *kote* strike.

As these figures would indicate, failure to perform *fumi-komi-ashi* correctly will naturally increase the likelihood of sustaining a heel injury. If this is to be prevented, *fumi-komi-ashi* must be executed at virtually the same time as the strike, and the entire sole of the foot should come into contact with the floor.

APPENDICES

A Kendo *shiai*

COMPETITION AND JUDGING

Although Kendo matches are bound by certain rules, these rules need not be restricting: it is more important that you act in accordance with your conscience. During a match, you must face your opponent with all your energy, but your actions should be ruled by your conscience. The referee judges the outcome of your actions—in other words, the effectiveness of a strike—a significant fact in the sense that the direction the match takes is influenced by this decision. This is why the referee's decision must be acceptable to both competitors and spectators. In this way, it is through competition that the essence of Kendo is expressed and its direction determined. For this reason, the referee is the key person controlling the direction of Kendo.

The Referee Must Be Fair

When judging a match the most important requirement is to be fair. In deciding victory or defeat, the referee must on no account be influenced by his personal feelings, based on past results or personal relationships with other referees. For example:

- If a prejudicial judgment is made based on past results, it puts one contestant at a disadvantage.

- If the referee is judging a friend or acquaintance, it is unfair. In such cases, it is better to switch with another referee as far as possible.

- The referee must not be influenced by the name of the school, *dōjō*, or company.

- The referee must not judge on the basis of his own preferences for certain kinds of *waza*.

Unfortunately, the above situations often occur, so it is important to focus exclusively on the two contestants at that particular moment, and no matter what, the outcome must be determined by what happens during that four- or five-minute bout. The opponents have only themselves to rely on in that ten meter square court and put everything they have into it. At the same time, the referee for his part must demonstrate a fair attitude when deciding on the outcome.

How Should the Strength of a Strike Be Judged?

In order to judge a Kendo match, the referee must first have reached a certain level himself through sufficient *keiko*. The judging of Kendo is most likely influenced to some extent by subjective elements. So, in addition to having a good theoretical grounding in Kendo and a thorough knowledge of the rules of judging, the referee must also have sufficient practical understanding of the types and difficulty of *waza* and opportunities for striking, and therefore personal experience of the relative strength of a strike.

When the referee is judging the relative strength of a strike, as he himself is not actually receiving the strike he cannot really know how it feels. He can only judge subjectively. The referee bases his judgment primarily on what he can see—in other words, where and how the strike was executed. To judge the relative strength of the strike the referee observes the course of the *shinai* and the place where a contestant is actually struck. The sound made by the strike is also taken into consideration. This means that if the eyes and ears of the referee are not functioning normally, he is not competent to be a referee.

Let us consider the different kinds of sounds heard during a match.

1. The sound of one *shinai* against another.
2. The sound made when the *men-buton* (cloth part of the *men*) or the *men-gane* (face guard) is struck.
3. The sound made when the *tsutsu-bu* (wrist) or the fist of the *kote* is struck, or when the *kote* is struck across the *tsuba* (guard on *shinai*).
4. The sound made when the *dō* is struck.
5. The sound of the player's voice.

A decision has to be made as to the effectiveness of the strike by judging these sounds in a single moment. This, combined with the fact that the sounds are often difficult to hear because of the supporting cheers of spectators and teammates, makes judging very difficult. In order to facilitate the referee's task and ensure that better judging takes place, spectators should refrain as far as possible from cheering the contestants.

Judging Is All or Nothing

Judging a Kendo match is a matter of making a declaration of valid or invalid. Even if a strike is very close to being valid, it will still be judged invalid. In such cases, zero points are scored and the referee must continue his task from square one. This is particularly important when we consider the two kinds of psychology that come into play for the referee after a strike which is close to being valid is executed. After such a strike, the referee may expect the next strike to be even better. Or he may focus more on the fact that a strike has just failed. When these tendencies come into play, the judging becomes unfair. This is why it is important for the referee to concentrate exclusively on the validity or invalidity of the strike being executed at that particular moment.

The Most Important Characteristic of a Cutting Edge Is to Be Able to Strike Correctly

Breaking with tradition leads to extinction, since tradition preserves the continuity of a people.

So how does this relate to Kendo? "Strike correctly with the cutting edge." If you fail to recognize this, Kendo becomes something devoid of meaning. For Kendo is not simply the donning of *keiko-gi* and *hakama*, putting on the armor, taking hold of the *shinai*, and striking an opponent. Even if you have no Kendo equipment other than the *shinai*, if you hold and use the *shinai* correctly, you are closer to true Kendo than someone in full equipment might be. In this sense, the tradition, the continuity of Kendo lies in "striking correctly with the cutting edge," and breaking with this tradition would spell the end of this sport.

In the following pages we have reproduced the official English-language rules and regulations as drawn up by the Japan Kendo Federation. No alterations other than minor typographical corrections and suchlike have been made to them.

THE REGULATIONS OF KENDO MATCH AND ITS REFEREEING
Subsidiary Rules of Kendo Match and its Refereeing
Guidelines for Kendo Match and its Refereeing

Revised April 1, 1995   JAPAN KENDO FEDERATION

REGULATIONS OF KENDO MATCH AND ITS REFEREEING
(Hereinafter referred to as "the Regulations")

INDEX

Part II SHINPAN (Refereeing)

Chapter 1 General Rules

Chapter 2 Refereeing

Section 1 Matters concerning Refereeing

Section 2 Disposition by Referees

Section 3 Matters concerning Conference or Protest

Chapter 3 Pronouncement and Flag Signals

Chapter 4 Supplement

Article 1 (Purpose of the Regulations)

The purpose of the Regulations is to get Kendo players to play fair at matches of the ALL JAPAN KENDO FEDERATION in accordance with the principles of Kendo and to properly referee the matches without prejudice.

Part I Match

Chapter 1 General Rules

Article 2 (Match Court)

The specifications of a match court are as follows, provided that, as a general rule, its floor shall be boarded:

1. The configuration of a match court should be a square or a rectangle with sides of 9 to 11 meters in length including the width of the line tape.

2. The center of the match court shall be marked by a cross, and two set lines shall be drawn on both sides of the center at the same distance therefrom. The length of the set lines and the distance between the lines are stipulated in the Subsidiary Rules.

Article 3 (SHINAI)

The SHINAI (Bamboo Sword) shall be made of bamboo or a synthetic material approved by ALL JAPAN KENDO FEDERATION as a bamboo substitute. The structure, length, and weight of the SHINAI and the specifications of the TSUBA (Hilt) are stipulated in the Subsidiary Rules.

Article 4 (Protectors)

KENDO-GU (Protectors) consists of MEN (Head Gear), KOTE (Fencing Gloves), DO (Plastron), and TARE (Waist Protector).

Article 5 (Costume)

The KENDO costume consists of KENDO-GI (Jacket) and HAKAMA (Skirt).

Chapter 2 Match

Section 1 Matters concerning the Match

Article 6 (Match Period)

The standard period time for a match is five minutes, and an extension period (ENCHO) is three minutes. The time from the pronouncement of YUKO-DATOTSU or suspension of the match made by Chief Referee (SHUSHIN) to the resumption of the match shall not be counted as part of match period.

Article 7 (Decision of Victory or Defeat)

Victory or defeat in a match shall be decided in accordance with the following rules:

1. Victory or defeat shall be decided generally in accordance with the SANBON-SHOBU (Three-point-scoring) rule; however, it may be decided in accordance with the IPPON-SHOBU (One-point-scoring) rule in case of management need at tournaments.

2. In SANBON-SHOBU, the first player to score two points within the match period shall gain a victory; however, if a player scores one point without conceding any points within the match period, the player shall also gain a victory.

3. When victory or defeat has not been decided within the match period, an extension (ENCHO) of the match may be allowed wherein the first player to score one point shall gain a victory.

   Otherwise, victory or defeat may be decided at the referees' judgment (HANTEI) or by lot, or the match may be pronounced a draw.

4. When victory or defeat of the match has been decided at the referees' judgment (HANTEI) or by lot, the winner shall be given one point.

5. When pronouncing HANTEI, referees shall take into consideration, first players' skill, then their attitudes in the match.

Article 8 (Team Match)

Team Matches shall be carried out in accordance with the following rules; however, the rules may be modified at respective tournaments if necessary.

1. The Team with the most winners shall gain a victory. When the number of winners turns out to be equal, the Team with the most points shall gain a victory. Furthermore, if the number of points scored is equal, two representative players from each Team shall fight to the finish.

2. In the case of the KACHINUKI method, a player of a Team who has defeated an opponent player may continue to fight against the next player as long as the winner keeps winning, and the Team which has defeated the last player of its opponent Team shall gain a victory.

Article 9 (Beginning and Ending of a Match)

Beginning and Ending of a Match shall be pronounced by the Chief Referee.

Article 10 (Suspension and Resumption of a Match)

Suspension of a Match shall be pronounced by Referees, and Resumption of a Match shall be pronounced by Chief Referees.

Article 11 (Request for Suspension of a Match)

If a player is unable to continue due to accident etc., the player may request a suspension of the Match.

Section 2 YUKO-DATOTSU

Article 12
(YUKO-DATOTSU (Effective Strike and Thrust))

YUKO-DATOTSU is defined as "an accurate strike or thrust made onto DATOTSU-BUI spot of the opponent's protector with the SHINAI at its DATOTSU-BU edge or point in high spirits and with correct posture; followed by ZANSHIIN (the state of alertness both mental and physical against the opponent's counterattack)."

Article 13 (DATOTSU-BU of the SHINAI)

The DATOTSU-BU of the SHINAI (the part of the SHINAI at which players should make YUKO-DATOTSU) is the JIN-BU (blade side opposite to the TSURU) of the MONOUCHI (one-third of the SHINAI from its point) and its neighboring part.

Article 14 (DATOTSU-BUI)

DATOTSU-BUI (strike targets) are as follows (see Fig. 3 in the Subsidiary Rules):

1. MEN (head spot) (forehead and the right and left head);
2. KOTE (forearm spot) (the right and left forearms);
3. DO (trunk spot) (the right and left sides of the plastron); and
4. TSUKI (throat spot) (TSUKI-TARE, throat protector).

Chapter 3 Prohibited Acts

Section 1 Matters relative to Prohibited Acts

Article 15 (Drug Abuse)

Players are prohibited from taking stimulating drugs.

Article 16 (Insult)

Players are prohibited from insulting utterances and acts against Referees or opponents.

Article 17 (Miscellaneous)

Players are prohibited from the following acts:

1. Use of protectors other than those admitted here in (Disallowed Protectors);
2. Tripping up or sweeping of the opponent's legs;
3. Unfairly shoving or pushing an opponent outside the match court;
4. Stepping outside the match court;
5. Dropping the SHINAI;
6. Requesting for suspension of the match without a justifiable reason; and
7. Doing other acts violative of the Regulations.

Section 2 Penalties

Article 18

A player who has committed a Foul Play prescribed in Articles 15 and 16 shall lose the match and be ordered to retire from the match area. The opponent shall be given two points. Any points or the preferred status gained by the offending player shall be totally nullified.

Article 19

A player who has committed the Foul Play stipulated in Article 17, Item 1 shall be subject to the following penalties. When both players have committed such Foul Plays, both shall lose the match and their points or preferred statuses gained in the match shall be nullified.

1. A player who has used a prohibited protector or SHINAI shall lose the match and any points or preferred status shall be nullified. The opponent shall be given two points.
2. The effect of penalty in the preceding paragraph is not retroactive to preceding matches wherein the use of the prohibited article had not been detected.
3. A player detected in such improper use shall be prohibited from continuing to play at remaining matches; however, the violator may play as a substitute at Team Matches unless otherwise provided at the tournament.

Article 20

1. When a player has committed a Foul Play stipulated under Article 17, Items 2 to 7 twice, the opponent shall be given one point. The number of such Foul Plays shall be cumulative during a match. However, in an extension or when both players have gained one point respectively, or if a second Foul Play is committed by both players

simultaneously, such Foul Plays shall be offset and not subject to penalty.

2. For the Foul Play stipulated in Article 17, Item 4: when both players have stepped out of the match court, the player who first committed the Foul Play shall be subject to penalty.

3. In the case of Article 17, Item 4: when a pronouncement of an effective strike or thrust has been revoked, the Foul Play shall not be subject to penalty.

4. For the Foul Play stipulated in Article 17, Item 5: when the opponent has made an effective strike or thrust immediately after the Foul Play, the Foul Play shall not be subject to penalty.

Part II Refereeing

Chapter 1 General Rules

Article 21 (Composition of Referees)

Referees shall consist of a Referee Director (SHIN-PAN-CHO), Presiding Referees (SHINPAN-SHU-NIN) (appointed only in case two match courts or more are set up), and Referees.

Article 22 (Referee Director)

The Referee Director shall have the necessary power to see that fair matches are secured.

Article 23 (Presiding Referee)

Presiding Referees shall assist the Referee Director with the power to control the matches at the respective match courts.

Article 24 (Referee)

1. Referees shall consist of a Chief Referee (SHU-SHIN) and two Subreferees (FUKUSHIN) having, as a general rule, equal powers to decide YUKO-DATOTSU and others.

2. The Chief Referee shall have the power to administer the match and make signals and pronouncement of YUKO-DATOTSU, HANSOKU (Foul Play), etc. by the motion of referee flags (hereinafter "flag").

3. The Subreferees shall assist the Chief Referee in the administration of the respective matches by making flag signals on YUKO-DATOTSU, HAN-SOKU, etc. Further, in case of emergency, the Subreferees may make signals and pronouncement of suspension of matches.

Article 25 (Court Staff)

With a view to properly managing matches, the Court Staff shall consist of time keepers, score board recorders, score recorders, and player callers. The composition and duties thereof are provided for in the Subsidiary Rules.

Chapter 2 Refereeing

Section 1 Matters concerning Refereeing

Article 26 (Decision on YUKO-DATOTSU)

A DATOTSU (Strike and Thrust) shall be concluded as YUKO (Effective) with one point scored in the following cases:

1. When two or three referees have made a signal of YUKO-DATOTSU; and

2. When one referee has made a signal of YUKO-DATOTSU and the other referees have made a signal of renunciation.

Article 27 (Revocation of YUKO-DATOTSU Pronouncement)

When a player has committed an improper act, the decision of YUKO-DATOTSU may be revoked upon referees' conference (GOGI) even after its pronouncement.

Article 28 (Mistakes in Decision on YUKO-DATOTSU)

If a Referee has entertained doubt about a decision on YUKO-DATOTSU etc., the Referee shall call a conference (GOGI) wherein Referees shall decide on the exception.

Article 29 (Manner of Refereeing)

Referees shall referee in the following manner:

1. When a Referee has made a signal of YUKO-DATOTSU, the other referees shall make immediate signals of their judgments.

2. When a YUKO-DATOTSU has been admitted or the match has been suspended, the Chief Referee shall direct the players to return to the center of the set lines and resume the match.

3. When a Referee has found a Foul Play, the Referee shall immediately suspend the match and make a flag signal to that effect. However, if the Foul Play was not obvious, a Referee shall call a conference (GOGI) wherein the Referees shall decide on the Foul Play.

4. When TSUBA-ZERIAI (Competing at TSUBA)

comes to a stalemate, the Chief Referee shall split both players on the spot and direct them to resume the match.

5. When a player has requested to stop the match, the Chief Referee shall pronounce suspension of the match and thereafter ask that player the reason.

6. When victory or defeat must be decided by HANTEI, all the Referees shall make a flag signal for the winner simultaneously with the pronouncement of HANTEI by the Chief Referee.

Section 2 Disposition by Referees

Article 30 (Injury or Accident)

When a player is unable to continue the match due to injury or accident, Referees shall dispose of the matter as follows, after hearing a cause thereof:

1. Referees shall determine on whether to continue the match or not after consulting with a medical doctor. As a general rule such a determination shall be made within five minutes.

2. In case a player is unable to continue the match due to injury: if the opponent has caused the injury, the opponent shall lose the match; but if the cause is unknown, the incapacitated player shall lose the match.

3. The player who has been treated as an incapacitated player due to injury or accident may be reinstated in remaining matches if a medical doctor and referees allow him or her to do so.

4. The player who has lost a match as an offender will not be allowed to play in the remaining matches.

Article 31 (Default)

A player who has defaulted a match shall become the loser and be prohibited from reinstatement in the remaining matches.

Article 32 (Points Scored for the Incapacitated or Defaulted Player)

The winner by virtue of Articles 30 or 31 shall be given two points, and the one point which has been scored by the Incapacitated Player shall remain valid. However, in an extension, the winner shall be given one point.

Article 33 (Points or Preferred Status of the Offender)

The points or preferred status of the Offender who has lost the match by virtue of Article 30, Item 2 shall be invalidated.

Section 3 Matters concerning Conference (GOGI) or Protest (IGI)

Article 34 (GOGI (Conference))

When a conference (GOGI) is deemed necessary, a Referee shall suspend the match and call a conference in the center of the match court.

Article 35 (IGI (Protest))

Nobody shall be allowed to protest against a HANTEI decision made by the Referees.

Article 36

In case the manager of a team has entertained doubt in the performance of the Regulations by Referees, the manager may file a protest with the Presiding Referee (SHINPAN-SHUNIN) or the Referee Director (SHINPAN-CHO) within the match period for the player concerned.

Chapter 3 Pronouncement and Flag Signals

Article 37 (Pronouncement)

Referees shall pronounce on Beginning, Ending, Resumption, Suspensions, Split, YUKO-DATOTSU, Victory or Defeat, GOGI (Conference), and Foul Play in the manner prescribed in the attached table. Referees may add reasons for the Pronouncement, if necessary.

Article 38 (Flag Signals)

Flag Signals by Referees shall be for Suspension, Split, YUKO-DATOTSU, Victory or Defeat, GOGI, and Foul Play in the manner prescribed in the attached table.

Chapter 4 Supplement

Article 39

In case of matters not provided for in the Regulations, Referees shall decide thereon at a conference, after consulting with the Presiding Referee or the Referee Director.

Bylaw

1. In case it is difficult to abide by the Regulations and the Subsidiary Rules because of the size or nature of a tournament, the tournament may be carried out in disregard of these provisions, provided that the purpose of the Regulations and the Subsidiary Rules are not infringed.

2. The Regulations shall come into full effect as of July 1, 1995.

(Attached Table) Pronouncement by Referees and Flag Signals

	Matters	Pronouncement	Flag Signals	Manner
Beginning	Beginning of a match	"HAJIME"	Flags at both sides	Fig. 1
Resumption	Resumption of a match	"HAJIME"	Same as above	Fig. 1
Suspension	Suspension of a match	"YAME"	Both flags raised straight above	Fig. 6
YUKO-DATOTSU	Decision of YUKO-DATOTSU	"MEN, KOTE, DO, TSUKI ARI"	Flag raised at 45° to one the side	Fig. 2
	Denial of YUKO-DATOTSU		Both flags waved crosswise with hands stretched down	Fig. 3
	Renunciation of judging		Both flags crossed with hands stretched down	Fig. 4
	Revocation of decision of YUKO-DATOTSU	"TORIKESHI"	Both flags waved crosswise with hands stretched down	Fig. 3
	Beginning of the second point	"NIHONME"	Lowering a raised flag	Fig. 2
	Beginning of the third point after a tie	"SHOBU"	Same as above	Fig. 2
Decision of Victory or Defeat	Decision of victory or defeat	"SHOBU-ARI"	Lowering a raised flag	Fig. 2
	Beginning of an extension	"ENCHO-HAJIME"	Flags at both sides	Fig. 1
	Victory with one point	"SHOBU-ARI"	Same as YUKO-DATOTSU	Fig. 2
	1. Pronouncing HANTEI	1. "HANTEI"	1. Same as above	Fig. 2
	2. Victory by HANTEI	2. "SHOBU-ARI"	2. Lowering a raised flag	Fig. 2
	Victory by Default	"SHOBU-ARI"	Same as YUKO-DATOTSU	Fig. 2
	A draw	"HIKIWAKE"	Flags crossed above forehead	Fig. 5
	Incapacitation in a match	"SHOBU-ARI"	Same as YUKO-DATOTSU	Fig. 2
	Victory or Defeat by lot	"SHOBU-ARI"	Same as above	Fig. 2
	Match by Representative Players	"HAJIME"	Flags at both sides	Fig. 1
GOGI	Calling a conference by a Referee	"GOGI"	Both flags raised in right hand	Fig. 8
	Signaling of its result		Flag Signals made by Chief Referee	Fig. 2
HANSOKU	Drug Abuse	"SHOBU-ARI"	Same as YUKO-DATOTSU	Fig. 2
	Uncourteous Utterance or Acts	"SHOBU-ARI"	Same as above	Fig. 2
	Use of Prohibited Equipment	"SHOBU-ARI"	Same as above	Fig. 2
	Tripping or Sweeping of opponent's legs	"HANSOKU ( ) KAI"	Flags obliquely down at one side and declaring the numbers of HANSOKU by fingers toward the violator	Fig. 9

	Matters	Pronouncement	Flag Signals	Manner
HANSOKU	Shoving or pushing the opponent out of the Match Court	Same as above	Same as above	Fig. 9
	Dropping the SHINAI on the floor	Same as above	Same as above	Fig. 9
	Request for a break without a justifiable reason	Same as above	Same as above	Fig. 9
	Foul plays simultaneously committed by both players	Same as above	Flags obliquely down at both sides	Fig. 10
	Miscellaneous violations of the Regulations	Same as above	Flags obliquely down at one side and declaring the numbers of HANSOKU by fingers toward the violator	Fig. 9
	Having committed Foul Plays twice	Indicating "HANSOKU NIKAI" by fingers and "IPPON-ARI"	Same as YUKO-DATOTSU	Fig. 2
	Applying offset	"SOSAI" and "ONAJIKU-SOSAI" after the second offset	Both flags waved crosswise with hands stretched down	Fig. 3
WAKARE	1. When a match has come to a stalemate	1. "WAKARE"	1. Holding both Flags straight forward	Fig. 7
	2. To have players continue the match	2. "HAJIME"	2. Lowering both flags	Fig. 7
Injury, Accident, Default	Incapacitation due to injury, accident, or default	"SHOBU-ARI"	Same as YUKO-DATOTSU	Fig. 2

Table 1 Specifications of SHINAI (ITTO-NO-KAMAE)

	Sex	Junior High School Student	Senior High School Student (also, non-students of the same age)	University Students and other adults
Length	Both sexes	Shorter than 114 cm	Shorter than 117 cm	Shorter than 120 cm
Weight	Male	Heavier than 425 g	Heavier than 470 g	Heavier than 500 g
	Female	Heavier than 400 g	Heavier than 410 g	Heavier than 420 g

Table 2 Specifications of SHINAI (NITO-NO-KAMAE)

	Sex	University Students and other adults	
		DAITO (longer sword)	SHOTO (shorter sword)
Length	Both sexes	Shorter than 114 cm	Shorter than 62 cm
Weight	Male	Heavier than 425 g	Between 280 and 300 g
	Female	Heavier than 400 g	Between 250 and 280 g

Fig. 1   Match court (Standard)

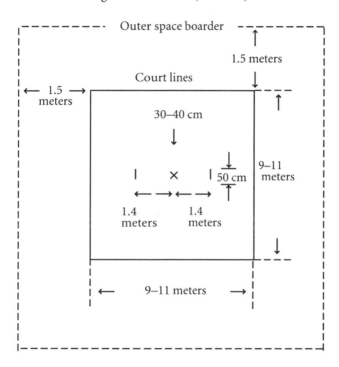

Fig. 2   Names of parts of SHINAI

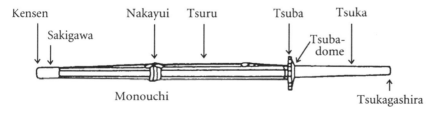

Fig. 3   KENDO-GU (Protectors) and DATOTSU-BUI
(Spots for strikes or thrusts)

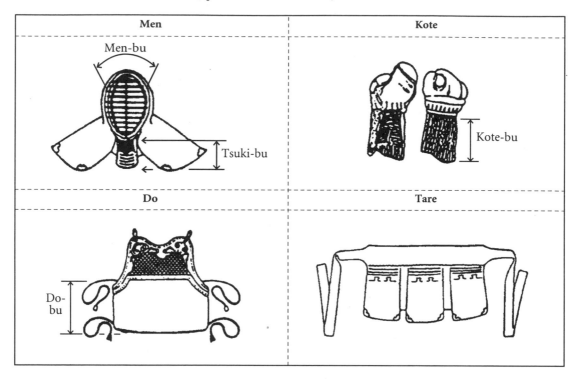

Fig. 4   Name tag of player

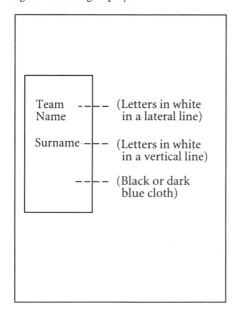

Fig. 5   Specifications of Referee Flags etc.

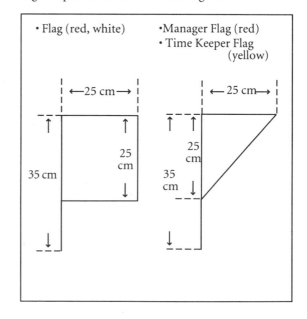

SUBSIDIARY RULES OF KENDO MATCH AND ITS REFEREEING

(hereinafter referred to as "the Subsidiary Rules")
Revised April 1, 1995 JAPAN KENDO FEDERATION

INDEX

Article 1

The specifications of a match court prescribed in Article 2 of the Regulations are as follows:

1. A space of at least 1.5 meters wide shall be kept outside the match court.

2. The width of the set line shall be 5 to 10 centimeters, and the color thereof shall be white as a general rule.

3. The cross in the center of the match court, the length of the set lines, and the distance between the lines are shown in Fig. 1.

Article 2

The specifications of the SHINAI referred to in Article 3 of the Regulations shall be as follows:

1. The SHINAI shall consist of four pieces of bamboo cut lengthwise or synthetic material and shall not include articles other than the core stuffed inside the SAKIGAWA (point cover) and the CHIGIRI (latching metal particle) inlayed at the end of the TSUKA (hilt). The names of the respective parts of the SHINAI are indicated in Fig. 2.

2. The specifications of the SHINAI are indicated in Tables 1 and 2. The length indicated refers to the total length of the SHINAI including all accessories, and the weight to the total weight including all accessories except the TSUBA (guard).

3. The TSUBA (guard) shall be round and made of leather or synthetic material. It shall not exceed 9 centimeters in diameter and must be fixed onto the SHINAI.

Article 3

KENDO-GU (Protectors) referred to in Article 4 of the Regulations are illustrated in Fig. 3.

Article 4

The match player shall wear a folded strip of cloth, either red or white, (total length of 70 centimeters and the width of 5 centimeters) at the crossing point of the DO strings on his or her back.

Article 5

The match player's name tag as illustrated in Fig. 4 must be affixed to the center piece of the TARE.

Article 6

The specifications of Referee Flags are shown in Fig. 5. The flag stick shall be 1.5 centimeters in diameter as standard.

Article 7

Match players may only wear supporters for medical reasons, provided that the supporters are not shabby or hazardous to their opponents.

Article 8

The manners of players in entering and leaving match courts may be specified at tournaments.

Article 9

HANTEI prescribed in Article 7, Item 5 of the Regulations shall be formed on the basis of the following criteria:

1. When a player has made a strike or thrust nearly equal to YUKO-DATOTSU, the player's skill should be regarded higher than otherwise.

2. When a player's posture and movements are predominant, the player's attitude should be regarded better than the other.

Article 10

The "accurate" strike prescribed in Article 12 of the Regulations means a strike made in the same direction as the true edge (JINBU) of SHINAI.

Article 11

The following DATOTSU (strikes or thrusts) shall be YUKO (effective):

1. DATOTSU made to the opponent immediately after the opponent has dropped his or her SHINAI;

2. DATOTSU made at the exact moment when the opponent has stepped outside the match court; and

3. DATOTSU made as the opponent falls down.

Article 12

DATOTSU in the following cases shall not be effective:

1. Two YUKO-DATOTSU have been made mutually and simultaneously (AIUCHI).

2. When a YUKO-DATOTSU is made, the opponent is checking the attacker by touching the latter's upper front body or protectors with the point of the former's SHINAI in high spirits and with correct posture.

Article 13

DATOTSU-BUI (strike targets) prescribed in Article 14 of the Regulations are shown in Fig. 3, and such spots of MEN and KOTE shall be specifically provided as follows:

1. The right and left head in MEN shall be above the temple.

2. The right spots of KOTE shall be the right forearm (the left forearm, if the opponent holds the SHINAI with his or her left hand forward) in the case of CHUDAN-NO-KAMAE) or the right and left forearms in the cases of the other KAMAE.

Article 14

Prohibited drugs prescribed in Article 15 of the Regulations shall be specified separately.

Article 15

"Stepping outside of the match court" prescribed in Article 17, Item 4 of the Regulations shall be specified as follows:

1. Having one foot totally outside the court line;

2. Having fallen on the floor with part of the body outside the court line; and

3. Supporting the body with part of the body or the SHINAI outside the court line.

Article 16

Prohibited Acts prescribed in Article 17, Item 7 of the Regulations shall include the following:

1. Putting one's hand on the opponent or holding the opponent in his or her arms;

2. Taking a hold of the opponent's SHINAI or taking a hold of his or her own SHINAI at its edge;

3. Holding the opponent's SHINAI in his or her arms;

4. Intentionally putting one's SHINAI on the opponent's shoulder;

5. After having fallen on the floor, the player lying on his or her face without counteracting the opponent;

6. Intentionally wasting time; and

7. Unfairly doing TSUBA-ZERIAI (competing at TSUBA) or unfairly making a strike or a thrust.

Article 17

The offset applied to the Foul Plays simultaneously committed as prescribed in Article 20 of the Regulations shall be implemented as follows:

1. In the case of the first Foul Play, the pronouncement thereof shall be first addressed to the player on the red side and thereafter to the player on the white side, followed by pronouncement of the offset.

2. In the case of the second or subsequent Foul Play, the pronouncement and the Flag Signals shall be made simultaneously.

Article 18

The duties of the Referee are as follows:

1. To strictly apply the Regulations and the Subsidiary Rules to matches;

2. To pay attention to the smooth progress of matches;

3. To render decisions on protests; and

4. To decide on matters which have not been prescribed in the Regulations or the Subsidiary Rules.

Article 19

The signals made by the Referee Director (SHINPAN-CHO) at the beginning of the first match shall be as follows:

1. In the case wherein one match court is set, the Referee Director (SHINPAN-CHO) shall stand up and direct the Chief Referee (SHUSHIN) to pronounce the beginning of a match, when the first players stand at RITSUREI (standing bow) (3 steps behind the set lines, hereinafter the same).

2. In the case wherein two match courts or more have been set, the Referee Director (SHINPAN-CHO) shall stand up and signal the beginning by whistle or the like, when all the first players stand at RITSUREI in unison.

Article 20

The duties of the Presiding Referee (SHINPAN-SHUNIN) are as follows:

1. To take responsibility for management of matches at the match court;

2. To pay attention to the proper application of the Regulations and the Subsidiary Rules;

3. To properly and promptly decide violations of the Regulations or the Subsidiary Rules and protests, if filed, and report to the Referee Director (SHINPAN-CHO), if necessary; and

4. To manage Referees in charge of the match court.

Article 21

The Duties of Referees are as follows:

1. To manage the respective matches;

2. To clearly pronounce and make signals;

3. To keep up smooth communication with the other Referees;

4. To acknowledge Flag Signals made by the other Referees; and

5. To reflect on his or her refereeing with other Referees (referring to the opinions of the Referee Director (SHINPAN-CHO) or the Presiding Referee (SHINPAN-SHUNIN), if necessary, after matches).

Article 22

The composition and duties of the Court Staff prescribed in Article 25 of the Regulations are as follows:

1. There shall be, in principle, one head time keeper and two or more subkeepers per court who shall keep the match time and make a signal at the end of the period of match time.

2. There shall be, in principle, one head recorder and two or more subrecorders per court who shall show the referees' pronouncements on boards and check referee flags.

3. There shall be, in principle, one head score recorder and two or more subrecorders per court who shall keep record of scores including points of YUKO-DATOTSU, number and type of HANSOKU, and the time spent for the matches.

4. There shall be, in principle, one head player caller and two or more subcallers per court who shall call players and inspect their equipment.

Article 23

The outfit of Referees is as follows, unless otherwise provided in the respective tournaments:

1. The jacket shall be of a dark blue color (plain).

2. The pants shall be of a gray color (plain).

3. The shirt shall be white (plain).

4. The neck tie shall be of a deep red color (plain).

5. The socks shall be of a dark blue color (plain).

Article 24

The revocation of YUKO-DATOTSU provided for in Article 27 of the Regulations shall be applied in the following cases:

1. When the player who made a YUKO-DATO-TSU is not on the alert both in spirit and posture for a possible counterattack by the opponent.

2. When a player who made a YUKO-DATOTSU

has made exaggerated gestures of surplus power or effectiveness of DATOTSU.

Article 25

The Mistakes in Decision on YUKO-DATOTSU provided in for Article 28 of the Regulations shall be the following cases:

1. In case an erroneous decision has been made in regard to the player who has made a YUKO-DATOTSU;

2. In case a decision on a YUKO-DATOTSU has been made in disregard of a signal for the end of the match time; and

3. In case a decision on a YUKO-DATOTSU has been made during a match period which should have terminated if the number of Foul Plays had been correctly calculated.

Article 26

"WAKARE" (split) provided for in Article 29, Item 4 of the Regulations shall be carried out as follows:

1. The Chief Referee shall split both players by pronouncing "WAKARE" and thereafter have them resume the match.

2. The spot where both players are split shall be within the match court.

Article 27

In case a Referee has found that a TSURU was not on the upside of the SHINAI, the Referee shall notify the Chief Referee of the impropriety and the Chief Referee shall clearly direct the player to correct it. Further, if the impropriety is repeated by the player, the Referees shall not admit a YUKO-DATOTSU for the player.

Article 28

The default provided for in Article 31 of the Regulations shall include the following case:

1. In case a player has arbitrarily defaulted the match for health or other reasons.

Article 29

The protest provided in for Article 36 of the Regulations shall be filed in the following manner before the time of SOGO-NO-REI (mutual bow) made by the players at the end of the match period:

1. The Manager shall make a signal for the filing of a protest.

2. The Manager shall state the contents of the objection to the Presiding Referee (SHINPAN-SHUNIN) or the Referee Director (SHINPAN-CHO).

GUIDELINES FOR KENDO MATCH AND ITS REFEREEING

Revised April 1, 1995   JAPAN KENDO FEDERATION

No. 1 Guidelines for players:

Players shall act in the following manner at the beginning and ending of a match.

(Entering or Leaving)

1. Upon entering into the court, players shall line up at their seats, give a REI to the main stand at the order of their Manager and take up their seats; likewise, prior leaving, they shall line up, give a REI and leave the court.

(The Line-up of a Team)

1. The two competing groups of players shall stand in a row facing one another (three steps behind the set lines) (See the Fig. 1 below) and conduct REI at the order of the Chief Referee. At the beginning, only SENPO (the first player) and JIHO (the second player) shall gird themselves with Protectors. In case the next match follows the ending one, two teams shall line up in a row. However, if two teams (starting and ending) cannot stand in a row like Fig. 1, the two ending teams and the two starting ones shall conduct REI separately (See Figs. 1 and 2 re. Line-up in Team Matches).

(REI to the Main Stand)

1. The REI to the main stand shall be conducted as follows in accordance with the instructions of the Chief Referee:

   (1) At the beginning of the first match, and at the beginning and ending of the final match of a tournament;

   (2) If the tournament runs for more than a day, at the beginning of the first match and at the ending of the last one of each day, further at the beginning and ending of the final match; and

   (3) The REI to the main stand shall be conducted at RITSUREI.

(The Beginning of a Match)

1. Prior to a start-up, the two competing players shall first proceed to the position of RITSUREI, exchange REI (REI in a standing posture) with SAGETO (holding SHINAI at the left side of the body), then take three steps forward, take SON-KYO position drawing SHINAI and stand up at the Chief Referee's announcement of HAJIME and then move into action.

(YUKO-DATOTSU)

1. The players shall stop the fight promptly upon the Chief Referee's pronouncement of YUKO-DATOTSU, return to the set lines and take CHUDAN-NO-KAMAE to receive the Chief Referee's pronouncement.

(Request for a break)

1. The player shall motion to the Chief Referee by raising a hand when the former requests a break during the fight and explain the reason for the request.

2. Players shall replace SHINAIs standing at the set lines, retreat inside the court lines and take SONKYO or sit in SEIZA when they correct regulations of equipment or apparel.

(Suspension)

1. In case a Referee has pronounced "YAME," the players shall immediately stop the match, and return to the set lines to receive the pronouncement or instructions of the Chief Referee.

(GOGI)

1. Upon the Chief Referee's pronouncement of GOGI, the players shall replace SHINAI while standing at the set lines, step back to the position inside the court lines and wait in SONKYO or SEIZA.

(Resumption)

1. For resumption of the fight after a break, the players shall take CHUDAN-NO-KAMAE at their set lines and resume the fight at the pronouncement of the Chief Referee.

(WAKARE)

1. Upon the Chief Referee's pronouncement of WAKARE, the players shall immediately separate from each other to take CHUDAN-NO-

KAMAE at that spot and resume playing the match upon pronouncement by the Chief Referee.

(Filing a Protest (IGI))

1. In case the manager has filed a protest (IGI), the players shall wait in the same manner as GOGI.

(HANTEI, CHUSEN-GACHI, Incapacitation)

1. In case of victory or defeat by HANTEI, the players shall stand at the set lines in CHUDAN-NO-KAMAE to receive the pronouncement by the Chief Referee.

2. In ease of victory or defeat by lot or incapacitation, the player shall act in the same manner as (1) above.

(FUSEN GACHI (Default))

1. When a player receives the pronouncement of FUSEN GACHI, he or she shall proceed to the set line in the same manner as that of beginning to stand up for the pronouncement, take SONKYO position again, replace SHINAI and retreat to the original position.

2. For a FUSEN GACHI pronouncement in a team match, the winning team shall stand in a row and receive the pronouncement. (See Fig. 1 re. Line-up of Team Matches)

(Ending)

1. At the end of a match, the players shall first return to their set lines, take CHUDAN-NO-KAMAE, receive the Chief Referee's announcement, take SONKYO position, replace SHINAI, stand up, take steps back in TAITO posture to the RITSUREI positions, lower SHINAI to SAGETO position and exchange a standing REI.

2. At the closing of a team match, the players of both teams shall line up at the RITSUREI position and retreat after exchanging REI upon instructions by the Chief Referee. On this occasion, the last player shall stand in line holding SHINAI and equipped with protectors. (See Fig. 1 and 2 re. Line-up of Team Matches)

(Other guidelines)
(NITO (two SHINAI) KAMAE and Replacing)

1. Players shall handle two SHINAI (NITO) in the following way:

   (1) Both DAITO (long SHINAI) and SHOTO (short one) shall be carried by the left hand in SAGETO.

   (2) In taking a KAMAE position, first the SHINAI to be held by the left hand shall be drawn by the right hand and passed to the left hand, then the second SHINAI in the left hand shall be drawn by the right hand for KAMAE.

   (3) For replacing the two SHINAIs, first the one in the right hand shall be replaced into the left hand and the second one in the left hand be replaced by the right hand.

   (4) The rest of the manner shall be the same as the case of ITTO (single SHINAI).

2. The costume of players shall be kept neat without rips or tears.

3. The protectors should fit tightly so as not to come loose during matches. In addition, the length of MEN strings shall be no more than 40 centimeters from the knot.

4. The players shall give only SOGO-NO-REI in match courts and refrain from bowing to the Referees or privately bowing to each other in sitting.

5. In case of change of players, players shall not shake hands or tap at the trunk of one's teammate.

6. Players shall refrain from entering the match court until Referees have stood at the set positions after moves.

7. A player shall not enter the match court before another player of the ending match has left the match court.

8. The managers or players shall not bring watches into the players' waiting area or make signals to or cheer a fighting player.

9. During the SENPO match or the final match, the waiting players are expected to sit in SEIZA.

Guidelines for Referees

(Entering)

1. When entering or leaving match courts, Referees with the Chief in the middle shall stand in line at the center inside the court lines holding the flags in the right hand (See Figs. 1 and 6 re. How to Move or Rotate Referees).

(Moves and holding of Flags prior to the Beginning of Matches)

1. Moves of Referees shall be as follows:

   (1) In the case of Individual Matches (the first

match), Referees shall move to the original position after the line-up (See Fig. 1 to Fig. 2 re. How to Move or Rotate Referees).

(2) In the case of Team Matches, Referees shall move to original positions after the line-up and the two teams have exchanged REI on the instructions of the Chief Referee (See Fig. 1 to Fig. 2 re. How to Move or Rotate Referees).

2. Holding of Flags by Referees shall be as follows:

(1) When moving, Referees shall hold the Flags in the right hand.

(2) After moving to the original position, the Chief Referee shall hold the red flag in his right hand and the white flag in his left hand, whereas a Subreferee shall hold the white flag in his right hand and the red flag in his left hand.

(3) When rotating, a Referee shall hold both flags with the white flag inside and the red flag outside.

(Rotation of Referees)

1. The rotation of Referees shall be done as follows (see Figs. 3 to 6 re. How to Move or Rotate Referees):

(1) (Rotation of Chief Referee and Subreferee)

The respective Referees shall move to the original position for rotation without settling flags (see Fig. 3)

(2) (Alternation of Referees at respective positions)

A Referee shall alternate with the succeeding Referee after settling flags and exchanging REI (see Fig. 4)

(3) (Alternation of one Referee after move)

The respective referees shall move to the original positions and the one who has finished refereeing as the Chief Referee, after settling flags, shall alternate with the succeeding Subreferee after exchanging REI (see Fig. 5).

(4) (Alternation of Referees who have finished refereeing)

The Referees who have finished refereeing, after settling flags, shall stand in a row and alternate with the succeeding Referees (see Fig. 6).

(REI to the main stand)

1. Referees shall conduct REI to the main stand in the following cases:

(1) At the beginning of the first match and at the beginning and ending of the final match; and

(2) When matches are held over two or more days, the REI shall be conducted at the beginning of the first match and the end of the last match of each day, and at the beginning and end of the final match.

2. The Chief Referee shall instruct REI to the main stand in the following cases:

(1) In the case of Individual Matches, immediately after Referees have stood at the original positions; and

(2) In the case of Team Matches, immediately after Referees and players have lined up.

(Beginning)

1. The Referee Director (SHINPAN-CHO) shall act as follows at beginning of the first match:

(1) When there is one match court, the Referee Director (SHINPAN-CHO) shall stand up when the first player stands in the RITSUREI position.

(2) When there are two or more match courts, the Referee Director (SHINPAN-CHO) shall stand up and make a signal by whistle or the like, when the first player stands in the RITSUREI position in unison with the others.

2. In having the first match start, the Chief Referee shall declare the beginning of the match after the signal of the Referee Director (SHINPAN-CHO) (see Fig. 1).

(YUKO-DATOTSU)

1. Flag Signals shall be made by Referees as follows (See Figs. 1 to 4 re. Flag Signals):

(1) When a YUKO-DATOTSU has been concluded, Referees shall return to the original positions holding flags as signaled and lower the flags upon pronouncement by the Chief Referee.

(2) When a YUKO-DATOTSU has not been concluded, Referees shall immediately stop signaling.

(3) When a Referee has made a Flag Signal indicating that a YUKO-DATOTSU should not be admitted, the Referee shall stop waving

the flags after having confirmed that the other Referees have acknowledged this signal (See Fig. 3 to Fig. 1 re. Flag Signals).

(4) When a YUKO-DATOTSU has been concluded, after the Chief Referee has made a signal denying a YUKO-DATOTSU or renunciation, the Chief Referee shall make a signal of YUKO-DATOTSU (See Figs. 3 and 4 to Fig. 2 re. Flag Signals).

2. In revoking a decision of YUKO-DATOTSU, the Chief Referee shall, after resuming the signals made prior to calling a GOGI, wave the flags crosswise after declaring the revocation (See Fig. 2 to Fig. 3 re. Flag Signals).

(Request for a break)

1. Upon acknowledgment of a player's request for a break, the Chief Referee shall immediately suspend the match and ask the player the reason for the request (Refer to Article 29, Item 5 of the Regulations).

2. When the Chief Referee has deemed the request for a break as unjustifiable, the Chief Referee shall call a conference (GOGI).

(Suspension)

1. A Referee shall pronounce suspension of matches in the following cases:

(1) Foul play;

(2) Injury or accident;

(3) To avoid dangers;

(4) When a player is unable to handle the SHINAI;

(5) Protest;

(6) GOGI (Conference); and

(7) When a TSURU is not on the upper side of the SHINAI.

2. Referees shall behave as follows when pronouncing a suspension (See Figs. 1 to 10 re. Flag Signals):

(1) Upon pronouncement of suspension, Referees shall return to the original positions.

(2) When both players have acknowledged the pronouncement of suspension or signals, Referees shall lower their flags (See Fig. 6 to Fig. 1 re. Flag Signals).

(3) When Referees have found a Foul Play, the Referees shall return to the original positions

holding the flag as signaled and lower the flag upon pronouncement to that effect by the Chief Referee (See Fig. 9 to 1 re. Flag Signals).

(4) When a Subreferee has pronounced suspension, the Chief Referee shall also pronounce suspension and make a Flag Signal (See Fig. 6 to Fig. 1 re. Flag Signals).

3. When a player has dropped his or her SHINAI or has fallen on the floor and the opponent has not made a strike or thrust, the Chief Referee shall suspend the match (See Fig. 6 to Fig. 1 re. Flag Signals).

4. When a Foul Play has been confirmed, the Chief Referee shall hold both flags in one hand and pronounce the kind and number of the Foul Play with a finger pointed to the violator and return to original posture (See Fig. 9 to Fig. 1 re. Flag Signals).

5. When both players have simultaneously committed Foul Plays and one point is to be given to the white (red) player, the Chief Referee shall pronounce it to the white player first, and then to the red player (vice versa) (See Fig. 10 to Fig. 1 re. Flag Signals).

(GOGI (Conference))

1. The conference of Referees shall be called in the following cases:

(1) Revocation of a decision on YUKO-DATOTSU;

(2) Mistake made by Referees;

(3) Unclear Foul Play; and

(4) Doubts on execution or application of the Regulations.

2. The conference shall be held by Referees as follows:

(1) The Chief Referee shall have both players retreat to inside the court lines.

(2) When a Subreferee has called a conference, the Chief Referee shall immediately suspend the match (See Figs. 6 and 8 to Fig. 1 re. Flag Signals).

(Resumption)

1. In the case of resumption for "NIHONME" (the second point) or "SHOBU" (fight to the finish), Subreferees shall lower the flags as signaled upon pronouncement thereof by the Chief Referee (See Fig. 2 to Fig. 1 re. Flag Signals).

2. In resuming the match after suspension, the Chief Referee shall behave in the same way as at the beginning of the match (See Fig. 1 re. Flag Signals).

(WAKARE (split))

1. When TSUBA-ZERIAI (competing at guards) has come to a stalemate, the Chief Referee shall have both split by holding flags straight forward upon pronouncement of "WAKARE," and resume the play by lowering flags upon pronouncement of "HAJIME" (See Fig. 7 to Fig. 1 re. Flag Signals). If a player is close to a court line, the Chief Referee may immediately adjust the positions of both players.

(Protest)

1. Referees shall handle protests in the following manner:

   (1) Referees shall immediately suspend the match (See Fig. 6 to Fig. 1 re. Flag Signals).

   (2) The Presiding Referee (SHINPAN-SHUNIN) or the Referee Director (SHINPAN-CHO) shall have Referees discuss on the protest at a conference (GOGI).

   (3) The Presiding Referee (SHINPAN-SHUNIN) or the Referee Director (SHINPAN-CHO) shall advise the manager of the result.

   (4) The Chief Referee shall resume the match (See Fig. 1 re. Flag Signals).

(Victory by HANTEI or Lot, or Incapacitation)

1. In deciding victory or defeat by HANTEI, Referees shall make a signal with their flags for the winner upon pronouncement of HANTEI by the Chief Referee (See Fig. 2 to Fig. 1 re. Flag Signals). On this occasion, Referees are not allowed to make a signal of tie or renunciation.

2. In pronouncing victory or defeat by lot or incapacitation, the Chief Referee shall make a signal for the winner upon pronouncement thereof and lower the flag instantly (See Fig. 2 to Fig. 1 re. Flag Signals).

(FUSENGACHI (Default))

1. For individual matches, the Chief Referee shall pronounce victory for the winner simultaneously with a Flag Signal (See Fig. 2 re. Flag Signals).

2. For team matches, the Chief Referee shall pronounce victory for the winner simultaneously with a Flag Signal after the winning team has lined up (see Fig. 2 re. Flag Signals).

(Ending)

1. When victory or defeat has been concluded or the match period has expired, the Chief Referee shall suspend the match and pronounce the conclusion simultaneously with a Flag Signal after the players retreat to the set lines (See Fig. 6–Fig. 1, Figs. 2 or 5–Fig. 1 re Flag Signals). Further, in the case of extension, the Chief Referee shall pronounce "ENCHO" and resume the match (See Fig. 1 re. Flag Signals).

2. When team matches have been terminated, Referees shall line up and the Chief Referee shall have both teams conduct REI with each other (See Fig. 1 re. Line-up in Team Matches).

(Miscellaneous)

1. Referees shall check if players wear their costume (KENDO-GI, HAKAMA, marking strips, and name tags) appropriately prior to the beginning of the match (Refer to Article 5 of the Regulations and Articles 4 and 5 of the Subsidiary Rules).

2. Referees shall check if players are equipped with appropriate protectors and SHINAI (including guard) (Refer to Articles 3 and 4 of the Regulations and Articles 3 and 4 of the Subsidiary Rules).

3. The Chief Referee shall correct inappropriate manners made by players.

4. The Referees shall strictly correct inappropriate utterances or acts made by players at players' seats after the matches.

5. The court staff shall carry out their duties by coordinating with the Presiding Referee or the Referee Director beforehand in order to smoothly administer matches.

6. Score board recorders shall put flags on Referees desks after checking them (six sets of flags per court are necessary).

LINE-UP MANNER IN TEAM MATCHES

Fig. 1 Line-up at the beginning and ending of the match (one team)

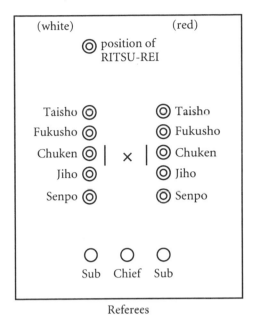

Fig. 2 Line-up at the beginning and ending of the match (two teams)

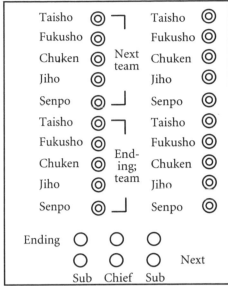

MOVES, ROTATION & ALTERNATION OF REFEREES

Fig. 1: Referees Row

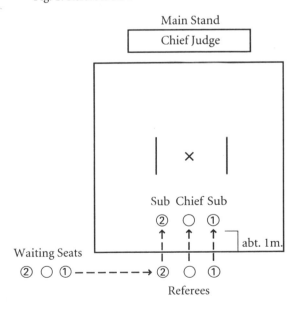

Fig. 2: Referees' Original Positions

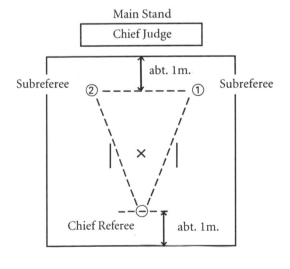

Fig. 3: Moves of Referees

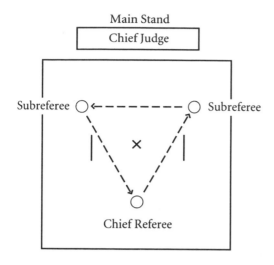

Fig. 4: Change of Referees

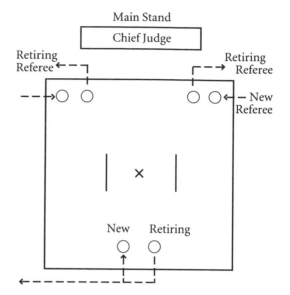

Fig. 5: Alternation of Subreferee

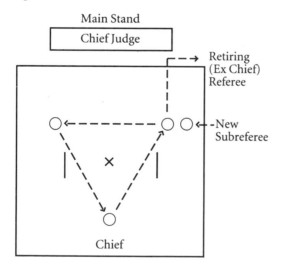

Fig. 6: Alternation in Group

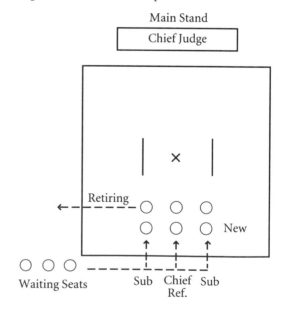

FLAG SIGNALS

Fig. 1   Beginning, Resumption, Ending
Flags at both sides (Standard posture)

Fig. 2   YUKO-DATOTSU, HANTEI, Decision of
Victory or Defeat
Raising a flag obliquely up on the side

Fig. 3   Denial or Revocation of YUKO-DATOTSU
or offset
Flags waved crosswise with hands stretched down

Fig. 4   Renunciation of Judging YUKO-DATOTSU
Flags crossed

Fig. 5   Draw
Flags crossed above forehead

Fig. 6   Suspension
Flags above shoulders

Fig. 7 WAKARE
Raising flags with both hands stretched straight forward

Fig. 8 GOGI
Raising flags straight above shoulder with the right hand.

Fig. 9 Foul Play
Holding a flag with the hand stretched obliquely downward to the side

Fig. 10 Simultaneous Foul Plays
Flags held with both hands stretched downward to both sides

Recording method

1. Recording matters and indications

Upon pronouncement by Chief Referee, recorders shall indicate the following marks on the recording board correctly to show the process of team match to Referees, players and audience.

Matters	Marks	Indications	Matters	Marks	Indications
YUKO-DATOTSU	M K D T	M = Men K = Kote D = Do T = Tsuki The order of recording of YUKO-DATOTSU shall be referred to those of Taisho match shown in Fig. 1 under.	Victory by lot	LOT	The word LOT shall be recorded for the victory by lot.
HANSOKU	▲	Foul plays shall be recorded as ▲ in red at the left side of either vertical end of the frame.	IPPON-GACHI	IPPON-GACHI	In case a player has gained one point without allowing the opponent points within the match period, the word IPPONGACHI shall be recorded.
HANSOKU Two Times	H	Where the second foul play is committed, the indication ▲ shall be deleted and the mark H be indicated on the opponent side.	ENCHO (extension)	ENCHO	In the case of an extension, the word ENCHO shall be put to the left side of the center line in the frame.
			Draw	×	In the case of draw, the mark × shall be put on the center line in the frame.
Offset		In offset, the mark of foul play shall be kept. The number of foul plays shall be recorded in the column opened in the recording paper.	FUSEN-GACHI Default Incapacitation	⌜○ ○⌟	The marks ○○ shall be put to the winner side, provided that the mark ○ shall be put to the same in the case of extension.
Victory by HANTEI	HANTEI	The word HANTEI shall be recorded for the victory by HANTEI.			

2. Recording method

(1) The recording method of the names of Referees, teams and players and of the marks are shown in Fig. 1.

Fig. 1 Recording board and recording method

Order	Senpo	Jiho	Chuken	Fukusho	Taisho	Referee
Team name	Player's name	Player's name	Player's name	Player's name	Player's name	Name of Chief Referee
Red	M			M	▲ M	—— The first point
					T	—— The third point
	IPPON-GACHI	ENCHO		×		Name of Subreferee / Name of Subreferee
White		HANTEI	○ ○	H	K	—— The second point
Team name	Player's name	Player's name	Player's name	Player's name	▲ Player's name	

(2) The recording method for individual matches shall be specified at the respective tournaments.

INTERNATIONAL KENDO

At present, Kendo is practiced in more than thirty countries worldwide. Some thirty-seven national federations and associations are affiliated with the International Kendo Federation, demonstrating the extent to which Kendo is enjoyed by all kinds of people outside Japan. Below, you will find a list of these federations and contact addresses for Kendo clubs in the United States, Canada, Australia, New Zealand, and the United Kingdom. More up-to-date information (particularly about purchasing Kendo equipment) can be obtained directly from the relevant organization in your country.

I.K.F. AFFILIATED ORGANIZATIONS

INTERNATIONAL KENDO FEDERATION
c/o Branch Office: NTT Bldg. 3-2-13
Kudan-kita, Chiyoda-ku, Tokyo 102

1. JAPAN
ALL JAPAN KENDO FEDERATION
2-3, Kitanomaru-koen, Chiyoda-ku
Tokyo 102

2. KOREA
KOREA KUMDO ASSOCIATION
Room #505 88 Olympic Center
Oryun-Dong, Songpa-Gu, Seoul

3. TAIWAN
REPUBLIC OF CHINA KENDO
ASSOCIATION
2F, No.261, SEC.3 Nan-King E. Rd.
Taipei, Taiwan

4. HONG KONG
HONG KONG KENDO ASSOCIATION
LIMITED
P.O. Box 25125
Harbour Building Post Office, Central

5. MALAYSIA
MALAYSIA KENDO FEDERATION
22, Jalan Setiajaya, Damansara Heights
50490 Kuala Lumpur

6. SINGAPORE
SINGAPORE KENDO CLUB
163-D Upper East Coast Road
Singapore 1545

7. THAILAND
THAILAND KENDO CLUB
84/5 Soi Raewadee 14
Tanon Tiwanon, Tambol Talad Kwan
Nontaburi 11000

8. AUSTRALIA
AUSTRALIAN KENDO RENMEI INC.
12 Rolland St, Coburg, Victoria 3058

9. NEW ZEALAND
ALL NEW ZEALAND KENDO
FEDERATION
P.O. Box 13545, Onehunga, Auckland 6

10. U.S.A.
ALL UNITED STATES KENDO
FEDERATION
P.O. Box 2004
Lomita, California 90717

11. HAWAII
HAWAII KENDO FEDERATION
1293 Ala Aloalo Street
Honolulu, Hawaii 96818

12. CANADA
CANADIAN KENDO FEDERATION
205 Riviera Dr. Unit #1, Markham
Ontario L3R 5J8

13. BRAZIL
ALL BRAZIL KENDO FEDERATION
Rua Valerio De Carvalho
63-Pinheiros
CEP 05422 São Paulo

14. ARGENTINA
FEDERACION ARGENTINA DE
KENDO
San Martin 1420, 3400 Corrientes

15. MEXICO
FEDERACION MEXICANA DE KENDO
Calle El Relox No.30, Col Chimalistac
C.P. 01070 Mexico D.F.

16. VENEZUELA
FEDERACION DE KENDO DE
VENEZUELA 7313
Poba International N° 100
P.O. Box 02-5255
Miami, FL 33102-5255 U.S.A.

17. GREAT BRITAIN
THE BRITISH KENDO ASSOCIATION
31 Woodstock Rise, Sutton
Surrey SM3 9JE

18. FRANCE
COMITE NATIONAL DU KENDO/FFJDA
43, Rue des Plantes
F-75680 Paris

19. SWEDEN
SWEDISH BUDO FEDERATION,
KENDO SECTION
Idrottens Hus
S-123 87 Farsta

20. BELGIUM
ALL BELGIUM KENDO FEDERATION
Rue Alphonse Helsen 30
B-6211 Mellet

21. NETHERLANDS
NEDERLANDSE KENDO RENMEI
Soeteliefskamp 20
NL-3343 EJ Hendrik-Ido-Ambacht

22. SWITZERLAND
SEKTION KENDO + IAIDO, SJF
Postfach 354
CH-4460 Gelterkinden

23. GERMANY
DEUTSCHER KENDOBUND, e.V.
(DKenB)
Heidenheimer Strasse 24
D-13467 Berlin-Hernsdorf

24. SPAIN
ASOCIACION ESPANOLA DE KENDO
Apartado de Correos N° 1399
E-07080 Palma de Mallorca

25. AUSTRIA
AUSTRIAN KENDO ASSOCIATION
Postfach 75, A-1033 Wien

26. NORWAY
NORGES KENDOFORBUND
Postboks 938 Sentrum
N-0104 Oslo

27. DENMARK
DANISH KENDO FEDERATION
Engvej 61 DK-2300
Copenhagen S.

28. FINLAND
FINNISH KENDO ASSOCIATION
Johtokiventie 3 C 18
SF-00710 Helsinki

29. ITALY
CONFEDERAZIONE ITALIANA
KENDO
Via Firenze 7
I-20025 Legnano (MI)

30. HUNGARY
HUNGARIAN KENDO ASSOCIATION
1111 Budapest
Lagymanyosi u.15. V/3

31. POLAND
POLISH KENDO COMMITTEE
Dereniowa 9 m 21
PL-02-776 Warszawa

32. YUGOSLAVIA
BELGRADE KENDO FEDERATION
Bircaninova 48
YU-11000 Beograd

33. ICELAND
ICELANDIC KENDO FEDERATION
Laugateigur 35
IS-105 Reykjavik

34. CZECH REPUBLIC
CZECH-MORAVIAN KENDO
ASSOCIATION
Krickova 1107
CS-16500 Praha 6-Suchdol

35. ROMANIA
ROMANIAN KENDO ASSOCIATION
C.P. 33-110, Piata Presei Libere 1,
RO-79738 Bucharest

36. SOUTH AFRICA
SOUTHERN AFRICAN KENDO
FEDERATION
38 Knox St. Waverley
SA-2090 Johannesburg

37. LUXEMBURG
LUXEMBURG KENDO CLUB
FLAM, Shobukai Kendo Luxembourg
B.P. 1258, L-1012 Luxembourg

DŌJŌS IN THE USA

ALASKA
Alaska Kendo Club
P.O. Box 201961
Anchorage, AK 99520

ARIZONA
Phoenix Kendo Kai
Desert West City Park
6501 W. Virginia
Phoenix, AZ 85035

CALIFORNIA
Bakersfield Kendo Dojo
2207 "N" St.
Bakersfield, CA

Chuo Kendo Dojo
Rafu Chuo Gakuen
202 N. Saratoga St.
Los Angeles, CA 90033

Costa Mesa Kendo Dojo
Higashi Buddhist Temple of
Newport Beach
254 Victoria
Costa Mesa, CA 92628

Covina Kendo Dojo
East San Gabriel Valley Japanese
Community Center
1203 W. Puente Ave.
West Covina, CA 91790

C.S.U.F. Kendo Dojo
South Gym: Rm #134
Cedar & Show Ave.
Fresno, CA

Gardena J.C.I. Kendo Dojo
Gardena Valley Japanese Cultural Institute
16215 South Gramercy Place
Gardena, CA 90247

Gardena Kendo Dojo
Gardena Valley Japanese Cultural Institute
16215 South Gramercy Place
Gardena, CA 90247

Hokushinkan Chiba Dojo California
5699 E. North Ave.
Fresno, CA 93725

Kings River Kendo Dojo
Kings River Community College
Reedley, CA

Long Beach Harbor Kendo Dojo
Long Beach Harbor Japanese Community
Center
1766 Seabright Ave.
Long Beach, CA 90810

Monterey Park Kendo Dojo
Sheriff's East LA Community Center
4360 Dozier
Los Angeles, CA

Mountain View Dojo
Mountain View Buddhist Temple
575 Stierlin Rd.
Mountain View, CA

Norwalk Kendo Dojo
Southeast Japanese Community Center
14615 S. Gridley Rd.
Norwalk, CA 90650

Oakland Kendo Dojo
DeFremery Center
1651 Adeline St.
Oakland, CA

Orange Co. Buddhist Church Kendo Dojo
Orange County Buddhist Church
909 S. Dale St
Anaheim, CA 92803

Palo Alto Kendo Dojo
2751 Louis Rd.
Palo Alto, CA

Pasadena Cultural Institute Kendo Dojo
Pasadena Japanese Cultural Institute
595 N. Lincoln Ave.
Pasadena, CA 91103

Sacramento Dojo
8320 Florin Rd.
Sacramento, CA

Salinas Dojo
Salinas Buddhist Temple
14 California St.

San Diego Kendo-Bu
c/o 3550 Winnetka Dr.
Bonita, CA 91902

San Diego Kendo Club
Ocean View United Church of Christ
3525 Ocean View Blvd.
San Diego, CA 92113

San Fernando Valley Kendo Dojo
San Fernando Valley Japanese
Community Center
8850 Lankershim Blvd.
Sun Valley, CA 91352

San Francisco Dojo
San Francisco Buddhist Temple
1881 Pine St.
San Francisco, CA

San Jose Dojo
San Jose Buddhist Temple
640 N. Fifth St.
San Jose, CA

San Jose State Univ. Kendo Club
Agnes Dev. Center
Monterrey & De La Cruz Rd.
Santa Clara, CA

San Mateo Dojo
King Center
825 Mt. Diablo Ave.
San Mateo, CA

Santa Barbara Kendo Dojo
Santa Barbara Buddhist Church
1350 Montecito St.
Santa Barbara, CA 93101

Sho-Tokyo Kendo Dojo
Hompa Hongwanji Temple Church Gym
815 East 1st Street
Los Angeles, CA 90012

Torrance Kendo Club
Torrance Cultural Arts Center
3330 Civic Center Dr.
Torrance, CA

Venice Kendo Club
Venice Japanese Community Center
12448 Braddock Dr.
Los Angeles, CA 90066

Watsonville Dojo
Watsonville Buddhist Temple
423 Bridge St.
Watsonville, CA

West Los Angeles Kendo Dojo
Sawtelle Japanese Institute
2110 Corinth Ave.
West Los Angeles, CA 90025

COLORADO
Colorado University Kendo Club
Carlson Hall Basement
Boulder, CO

Combat Art Center
Fort Collins, CO

Littleton Kendo Dojo
P.O. Box 3608
Littleton, CO 80161-3608

Mushinkan Kendo Club
US Air Force Academy
Colorado Springs, CO

Mushinkan Kendo Club
Aikido-kai Sanshinkan
3470-G Chelton Loop
Colorado Springs, CO 80909

Rocky Mountain Budokan
3427 South Broadway
Englewood, CO 80110

CONNECTICUT
Doshikan Greenwich Dojo
The Dundee Gymnasium
Mead School
55 Florence Rd.
Riverside, CT

First Yale Kendo Club
Yale University Gym
New Haven, CT

UCONN Kumdo Club
University of CT
Storrs, CT

DISTRICT OF COLUMBIA
Washington, D.C. Kendo Club
The Columbia Athletic Club
Columbia, MD

FLORIDA
Bradenton, Florida Dojo
6430 Lincoln Rd
Bradenton, FL 34202

Emerald Coast Kendo Club
c/o 12 Bay Ct. NE
Ft Walton Beach, FL 32542

Shidogakuin Miami Kendo Club
3825 County Line Rd.
Pembroke Park, FL 33023

GEORGIA
Georgia Kendo Alliance
Chastain Memorial Park Gym
Wiecca Blvd.
Atlanta, GA

Georgia Kendo Alliance
Lindley Middle School
Atlanta, GA

N.E. Atlanta Kendo Dojo
c/o 1441 Berry Cove Circle
Lawrenceville, GA 30243

Peachtree City Kendo Club
Glenloch Rec Center
c/o 629 Grecken Green
Peachtree City, GA 30269

University of Georgia Kendo Club
230 B Russell Hall
Athens, GA 30609

HAWAII
Ainakoa Shiseikan
Ainakoa District Park
c/o 1859-A Mahana St.
Honolulu, HI 96816

Aiea Taiheiji
Soto Mission of Aiea
99-045 Kauhale St.
Aiea, HI 96701

Honbu Dojo
Kaimuki Recreation
3521 Waialae Ave.
Honolulu, HI 96816

Kahului Kendo Club
291 So. Puunene Ave.
Kahului, HI 96732

Kenshi-kan Kendo Club
Japanese Cult. Center of Hawaii
2454 So. Beretania St.
Honolulu, HI 96814

Ken Yu Kai Kendo Club
Japanese Cultural Center of Hawaii
2454 So. Beretania St.
Honolulu, HI 96814

Mililani Kendo Club
Mililani District Park
94-200 Lanikuhana Ave.

Mililani, HI 96789
Myohoji Mission
2003 Nuuanu Ave.
Honolulu, HI 96817

Wahiawa Hongwanji
1067 California Ave.
Wahiawa, HI 96789

Waipahu Konkokyo
94-106 Mokukaua St.
Waipahu, HI 96797

Waipahu Seibukan
Pearlridge Elementary School Cafeteria
c/o 99-051 Ieie Pl.
Aiea, HI 96701

Hilo Hongwanji
398 Kilauea Ave.
Hilo, HI 96720

Hilo Kobukan
Hilo Recreation
c/o 41 Halenani St.
Hilo, HI 96720

IDAHO
Idaho Kendo Kai
Boise YMCA
Boise, ID

ILLINOIS
Chicago Kendo Dojo
Buddhist Temple of Chicago
1151 West Leland Ave.
Chicago, IL 60640

Choyokan Kendo Dojo
Japan Cultural Center
1016 West Belmont
Chicago, IL 60657

Moline Kendo Dojo
c/o 1201 5th Ave.
Moline, IL 61625

Normal Kendo Dojo
c/o 100 N. Diamond-Star Prkwy.
Normal, IL 61761

LOUISIANA
New Orleans Kendo Dojo
c/o 910 S. Carrollton Ave. Apt #J
New Orleans, LA 70118

MARYLAND
NIH Shidogakuin
Bldg 10, 14th floor gym
9000 Rockville Pike
Bethesda, MD 20892

MASSACHUSETTS
Acton Kendo Club
245 Main St.
Acton, MA 01720

Boston Kendo Kyokai
Church of Our Savior
25 Monmouth St.
Brookline, MA 02143

Boston Univ Kendo Assoc.
775 Commonwealth Ave.
Boston, MA

New England Kendo Assoc. (Medford)
Medford High School
Medford, MA

New England Kendo Assoc. (Natick)
25 Washington St.
Natick, MA

MICHIGAN
Battle Creek Kendo Kai
West Dickman Fitness Center
2851 West Dickman Rd.
Battle Creek, MI

Kyoshinkan MSU Kendo Club
1732 A Huntsville Dr.
Michigan State University
East Lansing, MI 48824-1321

MINNESOTA
Minneapolis Kendo Dojo
McCalister College Kendo
Minneapolis, MN

Rochester Kendo Club
c/o 626 E. Center St. #22
Rochester, MN 55904

MONTANA
Big Sky Kendo Kai
St. Paul's United Methodist Church
505 Logan
Helena, MT

NEBRASKA
Jinbukan
University of Nebraska
School of Health, P.E. & Recreation
Lincoln, NB 69599

Kenyu Kai
Chadron State College
Physical Activity Center
Chadron, NB

NEW JERSEY
Fort Lee Kyudokan Dojo
Dwight-Englewood School
315 East Palisades Ave.
Englewood, NJ

Korean Kum Do Assoc. USA
Hwa Rang Sang Moo Kwan
33 Country Rd.
Tenafly, NJ 07670

Korean Kum Do Assoc. USA
Kom Bop Sang Moo Kwan
424 Hillcrest Ave.
Palisade Park, NJ 07650

Korean Kum Do Assoc. USA
Hwang Yong Sang Moo Kwan
2 East Madison Ave.
Du Mont, NJ 07628

Shidogakuin Hakushikan
New Jersey
c/o 252 Lafayette St. #2E
New York, NY 10012

NEW MEXICO
New Mexico Kendo Dojo
c/o 629 Parkside Place SE
Albuquerque, NM 87123

Taos Kendo
P.O. Box 2868
Taos, NM 87571

NEW YORK
All Hallows HS Kendo Club
111 East 164th St.
Bronx, NY 10452

Colgate Kendo Club
Huntington Gym
Colgate University
Hamilton, NY

Cornell Kendo Club
MSC/18 Clark Hall
Cornell University
Ithaca, NY 14853

Doshikan Kendo Club
252 Lafayette St. #2E
New York, NY 10012

Soundance Studio
385 Broadway
New York, NY

Hartsdale Kyudokan Dojo
Woodlands H.S. Gym
475 West Hartsdale Ave.
Hartsdale, NY

Japanese Swordsmanship Society
Japanese Martial Arts & Cult. Academy
P.O. Box 1116
Rockefeller Center Stn.
New York, NY 10185

Ken Zen Institute
Japanese Martial Arts and Cult. Academy
152-8 West 26th St.
New York, NY 10001

Kongokan Dojo
735 Port Washington Rd.
Port Washington, NY

Korean Kum Do Assoc. USA
Central Sang Moo Kwan
8 Hillcrest Ave.
Manhasset, NY 11030

Korean Kum Do Assoc. USA
South Sang Moo Kwan
157-70 Northern Blvd.
Flushing, NY 11354

Korean Kum Do Assoc. USA
Meitokukan
The Loft
286 Central Ave.
Albany, NY

Mugen Dojo
Yanagi Martial Arts Dojo
283 Main St.
Farmingdale, NY 11735

New York City Kendo Club
Jan Hus Church
351 E. 74th St.
New York, NY 10021

Northern Westchester Kendo Club
Yorktown Community and Cultural
Center
1974 Commerce St.
Yorktown Heights, NY

Yushinkan
Marymount College
100 Marymount Way
Tarrytown, NY 10591

NORTH CAROLINA
Charlotte Kendo Club
Carolina Gymnastics & Martial Arts
14017 E. Independence Blvd.
Matthews, NC 28105

OHIO
Cleveland Kendo Association
Cleveland State University
Cleveland, OH

Miami Valley Kendo Club
601 E 5th St.
Dayton, OH

United States Classical Kendo Federation
1182 Thurell Road
Columbus, Ohio 43229

OREGON
Monmouth Kendo Club
Western Oregon State University
c/o 1243 Madrona Ave
Monmouth, OR 97361

Obukan Kendo Club—Eastside Dojo
Vikki Mills Dance Studio
3536 SE 26th
Portland, OR

Obukan Kendo Club-Hombu Dojo
Greenburg Plaza Jazzercise
10855 SW Cascade Blvd.
Tigard, OR

PENNSYLVANIA
Tan Shin Kai Kendo Dòjo
Community Education Center
3500 Lancaster Av.
Philadelphia, PA

Shinbu Kan Dojo
Lower Bucks Shotokan Karate Dojo
156 Fallsington Ave.
Tullytown, PA

Shu Do Kan Dojo
c/o 2716 Columbia St.
Easton, PA 18045

Rei Mei Kan Dojo
c/o 5932 Keystone Dr
Bath, PA 18014

SOUTH DAKOTA
South Dakota Kendo Club
3326 Harmony Ln.
Rapid City, SD 57702

TENNESSEE
JC Martial Arts Academy
2500 Wesley Street
Johnson City, TN

Memphis Kendo Dojo
Raleigh Community Center
c/o 4638 Talley
Millinton, TN 38053

Meiji Gakuin Kendo Club
1314 Peachtree St.
Sweetwater, TN 37874

TEXAS
Austin Kendo Doshikai
c/o 112 Franklin Blvd
Austin, TX 78751

Chubei at Denton
612 Hercules
Denton, TX 76201

Dallas-Fort Worth Kendo & Iaido Kyokai
Sammons Center for the Arts
Dallas, TX

Dance Traxx, Inc.
1422 Prestion Forest SQ
Dallas, TX

Hokushin Chiba Dojo
4230 Mangum
Houston, TX 77092

Texas Tech Kendo Club
Texas Tech Recreation Center
Lubbock, TX

University of Texas Kendo Association
University of Texas, Austin
Austin, TX 78713

UTAH
Ogden Kendo Club
Weber State University
Swanson Gymnasium, Rm. 19
Ogden, UT

USA Keishin Kan
15 South Main
Tooele, UT 84074

Utah Kendo Dojo
University of Utah
Health, P.E. & Rec., Room W105
Salt Lake City, UT

VIRGINIA
Blacksburg Kendo Club
Blacksburg YMCA
Blacksburg, VA

Waynesboro YMCA Kendo Club
Waynesboro, VA

WASHINGTON
Bellevue Kendo Club
Bellevue Parks Dept.
Highland Community Center
14224 Bel-Red Rd.
Bellevue, WA

Cascade Kendo Kai
Mercer View Community Center
8236 S.E. 24th St.
Mercer Island, WA

Highline Kendo Kai
1321 SW 102nd St.
Seattle, WA

Northwest Kendo Club
1600 Armory Way
Seattle, WA

Renton Community Center
1715 Maple Valley Hwy
Renton, WA

Seattle Kendo Kai
St. Peters Episcopal Church Gym
1610 S. King St.
Seattle, WA

Tacoma Kendo Club
1602 S. K St.
Tacoma, WA

Spokane Kendo Club
1528 S Maple
Spokane, WA

University of Washington Kendo Club
HEC Ed Pavilion Addition Gym
c/o 20825 6th Ave S.
Des Monies, WA 98198

WISCONSIN
University of Wisconsin Kendo Club
c/o 4859 Sheboygan
Madison, Wisconsin 53705

WYOMING
Cheyenne Budokan
5001 Griffith Ave.
Cheyenne, WY 82009

DŌJŌS IN CANADA

BRITISH COLUMBIA
Renbu Kendo Club
6535 East Broadway
Burnaby, B.C. V5B 2Y6

University of Victoria Kendo Club
Dept. of Biology
Box 1700
University of Victoria
B.C. V8W 2Y2

Vancouver Kendo Club
1649 Ralph Street
N. Vancouver, B.C. V7K 1V6

Steveston Kendo Club
4111 Moncton St.
Richmond, B.C. V7E 3A8

U. B. C. Kendo Club
8013 Hunter Street
Burnaby, B.C. V5A 2BS

Sunrise Kendo Club
6855 Adair St.
Burnaby, B.C. V5B 2W8

Shin Ken Kai Dojo
#303-2255 Eton St.
Vancouver, B.C. V5L 1C9

ALBERTA
University of Calgary Kendo Club,
#32 601 Dalton Dr., N.W.
Calgary, Alberta

Mr. Shaun Brookes
236 Silver Crest Dr., N.W.
Calgary, Alberta T3B 3A4

SASKATCHEWAN
Saskatoon Y.M.C.A. Kendo Club
2117 York Ave.
Saskatoon, Sask. S7J 1H7

MANITOBA
Manitoba Kendo Club
c/o Manitoba Japanese Canadian Cultural
Centre
180 McPhillips St.
Winnipeg, Man. R3E 2J9

ONTARIO
Etobicoke Kendo Club
1407 Shawson Drive
Mississauga, Ont. L4W 1C4

Burlington Kendo Club
28 Harper St.
Waterdown, Ont. L0R 2H3

J.C.C.C. Kendo Club
Japanese Canadian Cultural Centre
123 Wynford Drive
Don Mills, Ont. M3C 2Z4

Ottawa Kendo Club
5 Melrose Ave.
Ottawa, Ont. K1Y 1T8

Owen Sound Kendo Club
1350-16th St. East
Owen Sound, Ont. N4K 6N7

Renbu-Kan Kendo Club
75 Gillin Rd.
Brantford, Ont. N3P 1X2

Toronto Kendo Club
621 Tedwyn Dr.
Mississauga, Onc. L5A 1K3

Tillsonburg Kendo Club
49 Rolph St.
Tillsonburg, Ont. N4G 3X9

University of Guelph Kendo Club
(Sei-Do-Kai)
Dept. Anima Science
Guelph, Ont. N1G 2W1

University of Toronto Kendo Club
93 DeLoraine Ave.
Toronto, Ont. M5M 2B1

University of Waterloo Kendo Club
P.A.C. 2040
University of Waterloo
200 University Ave. W.
Waterloo, Ont. N2L 2G1

Yugen Kan DoJo
3816 Dominion Road
Ridgeway, Ont. L0S 1N0

McMaster Kendo Club
23 Nellingan Place
Hamilton, Ont. L8K 4X6

QUEBEC
Club de Kendo Isshin Montreal
10167 De St-Firmin
Montreal, P.Q. H2B 2G6

Kebekendo
120 Rue De Bernieres
Quebec P.Q. H3H 2P2

Quebec Kendo Kai
3103 Av. des Hotels, Suite 705
Ste. Foy, Quebec, G1W 4W6

McGill University Kendo Club
430 Rue Gohier
Saint Laurent, P.Q. H4P 1V5

Shido-Kan Kendo Club
c/o Tristar Gym
4058 Jean Talon W. #256
Montreal, P.Q. H4P 1V5

University of Montreal Kendo Club
7085 Rue Delanaudiere Apt. 4
Montreal, P.Q. H2E 1Y1

PRINCE EDWARD ISLAND
Fudoshin Kai
30 McKay Dr.
Charlottetown, P.E.I. C1A 5W3

DŌJŌS IN THE UNITED KINGDOM

LONDON
Hagakure Kendojo
The Beomund Centre
177Abbey Street
London SE1 2AN

Kenseikai
London Goju Karate Centre
53 Curtain Road
London EC2A

Nenriki
Geoffrey Chaucer School
Harper Road, Elephant and Castle
London

Univ. of London Kendo Bu
University College London
Bloomsbury Theatre
Gordon Street, Euston

Kenseikai (Tower Hamlets)
Langdon Park S. Centre
Byron Street, Poplar
London E14

Wakaba Kendo Club
Haverstock School
Chalk Farm Road, Chalk Farm
London NW1 8AS

Jugokan
Yawara Centre
205 Merton Road
Southfields
London SW18 5EE

Mumeishi
Cranford Community School
High Street, Cranford
Hounslow TW5 9PD

BERKSHIRE
Reading Kendo Club
YMCA
Parkside Road, Reading
Berkshire

BUCKINGHAMSHIRE
Gyosei International School
Japonica Lane
V10 Brickhill Street
Willen Park
M'Keynes

Kodokan
Simpsons Leisure Centre
High Wycombe
Bucks

CAMBRIDGESHIRE
Tsurugibashi Kendokai
Cambridge University
Cambridge

CHESHIRE
K.N.M.S.
Bramhall Recreation Centre
Seal Road, Bramhall, Nr Stockport
Cheshire

CORNWALL
Kenseikai (Falmouth)
Peryn School
Poltisho Road
Peryn
Cornwall

Kenseikai (St Austell)
St. Stephen in Brannel Secondary School
St. Austell
Cornwall

Kenseikai Cornwall
Beacon Village Hall
Camborne
Cornwall

DURHAM
Ni-Jo
Park View School
North Lodge
Chester-le-Street
Durham

University of Durham
East Gym College of St Hilda & St B
University of Durham
Durham

DORSET
Eishinkan (Dorset)
Holt Village Hall
Holt, Wimbourne
Dorset

GLOUCESTERSHIRE
Cheltenham & Glos College
Hardwick Campus
St Pauls Road
Cheltenham, Glos GL50 4BS

Shudokan
YMCA
Victoria Walk
Cheltenham, Gloucestershire

HERTFORDSHIRE
Ken Yu Kan
Stevenage Leisure Centre
Lytton Way, Stevenage
Herts. SG1 1SZ

KENT
Hatamoto Kendo Kai
St Peters Church
Trafalgar St, Gillingham
Kent ME7 1LD

Kyo Shin Kendo Kai
Our Lady of Gillingham
Ingram Road
Gillingham, Kent

Romney Marsh Kendo Kai
Lydd Junior School
Skinner Road
Lydd, Kent

Shinbukan-Tunbridge Wells
Sherwood Park CPS
Greggswood Road
Tunbridge Wells, Kent

UKKC
University of Kent S/Cent
Canterbury, Kent CT2 7NL

LANCASHIRE
Aka Bara
Sports Centre
Barlow Street
Rochdale, Lancashire

LEICESTERSHIRE
Gakushijuku
Marlene Reid Centre
Belvoir Road
Coalville, Leics

Gakushinjuku
Fullhurst Comm. Col
Imperial Avenue
Leicester

MERSEYSIDE
Yoshinkan
John Moores University
Mosley Hill Road
Liverpool

MIDLANDS
Masamune
Small Heath Comm. Centre
Munts Street, Small Heath
Birmingham

Nagamitsu Ken Kai
Small Heath Leisure Centre
Muntz Street
Birmingham

NORFORK
Seikukan
Oriental Arts Centre
Unit 18, St. Mary's Works
Duke Street
Norwich

NORTHUMBERLAND
Blyth Kendo Club
Cambous Welfare
Cambous, Blythe
Northumberland

Cullercoats Kendo Club
C.C.A. Hall
Belle Vue Street, Cullercoats
Northumberland NE30

NOTTINGHAMSHIRE
Kashi No Ki Ken Yu Kai
Dukeries Recreation Centre
New Ollerton
Nottinghamshire

OXFORDSHIRE
Syo Jin Kai
Temple Heath Fitness Club
109 Oxford Road, Cowley
Oxford

Hakuba Kai
Old Gaol Leisure Centre
Bridge Street, Abingdon
Oxford

PEMBROKESHIRE
Haverfordwest Dojo
Pembrokeshire College
Haverfordwest
Pembrokeshire SA61 1SZ

SOMERSET
Shiroishi
Whitstone Community School
Shepton Mallet
Somerset BA4 5PF

Tsunami
23 Reed Close, Watchet
Somerset TA23 0EF

STAFFORDSHIRE
Kagami Shin Kendo Kai
Willfield/ Queensbury C/Cn
Lauder Place, South Betilee
Stoke-on-Trent

SUFFOLK
Shi-Tennoji School
Herringswell Manor
Hermingswell, Bury St Edmunds
Suffolk 1P28 6SW

SUSSEX
Shinbukan B B Heath Leisure
Centre
Wickhurst Lane
Broadbridge Heath
Horsham

TYNE & WEAR
Shiro
Mortimer Comm. Assoc.
Mortimer Rd, South Shields
Tyne & Wear

YORKSHIRE
Doshinkenyukai
4 Ridgeway
Queensbury
Bradford BD13 2RE

SCOTLAND
Taiseidokai (Edinburgh)
Moray House, P.E. Centre
Holyrood Road, Edinburgh

Torii Kendo Club
Summerton Comm. Centre
Broomloan Road, Govan
Glasgow

DŌJŌS IN AUSTRALIA

Australian National University
Kendo Club
113 Dumas St
McKellar ACT 2617

Sydney Kendo Club
7/44-46 Hunter St
Hornsby NSW 2077

Central Coast Kendo Club
2 Roslyn St
Springfield NSW 2250

Wollongong University Kendo Club
PO Box 56
Buxton NSW 2571

Kenshinkai
4 Habana St
The Gap Qld 4061

Ballarat Kendo Club
17 Brown's Pde
Wendouree Vic 3355

Goshin Kendo Club
5/38 Verdant Ave
Toorak Vic 3142

Fudoshin Kendo Club
523 Heidelberg Rd
Alphington Vic 3078

Melbourne Kendo Club
(Kenshinkan Dojo)
91 Rooslyn St
West Melbourne Vic

Monash University Kendo Club
2/3 Verdant Ave
Toorak Vic 3142

University of Melbourne
Kendo Club
36 Park Grove
Richmond Vic 3121

University of Adelaide
Kendo Club
21 Thorngate Drive
Belair SA 5052

Budokan Academy
Lot 55 Nicholson Rd
Canningvale WA 6155

DŌJŌS IN NEW ZEALAND

Auckland Kendo Club
PO Box 13545
Onehunga
Auckland

Wellington Kendo Club
Victoria University of Wellington
PO Box 600
Wellington

GLOSSARY

ai-chūdan	both players in *chūdan-no-kamae*
ashi-sabaki	footwork
ayumi-ashi	walking step
bokken	wooden sword
bokutō	wooden sword
chigawa	loop on either side of the plastron
chūdan-no-kamae	middle guard position
daimyō	feudal lord
datotsu	strike or thrust
debana-waza	technique to execute a strike as your opponent is about to strike
dō	body, plastron; strike target
gedan-no-kamae	lower guard position
hakama	skirt
hasaki	cutting edge
hassō-no-kamae	guard position with the *shinai* held vertically at one's right side
hidari	left
hiki-waza	stepping-back technique
hiraki-ashi	sideways step
hirauchi	strike with the flat of the *shinai*
honshitsu	essence
irimi	fundamental short-sword guard position: action of stepping into your opponent's *maai*
issoku ittō no maai	distance at which one can attack (or avoid attack) in one step
jigeiko	free practice
jōdan-no-kamae	upper guard position
kaeshi-waza	reflex deflection technique
kakarigeiko	all-out attack practice
kamae	guard position
katana	sword
katsugi-waza	"shouldering the sword" technique
keiko	practice
keiko-gi	jacket
kendōgu	armor
kenjutsu	the art of the sword
kensen	point of sword or *shinai*
ki	spirit, mental energy
kiai	projection of fighting spirit into a voice or cry
kigurai	bearing, pride, dignity
kihaku	spirit
kirikaeshi	continuous strikes of right and left *men* alternately
kisei	spirit, vigor
kobushi	fist
kodachi	short sword
kote	gloves; forearm; strike target
maai	fighting distance between two opponents
men	headgear, mask; strike target
men-buton	cloth part of *men*
men-gane	grill part of *men*
metsuke	point of observation
migi	right
nidan-waza	two-stage technique
nōtō	resheathing the sword
ōji-waza	counter-attacking technique
okuri-ashi	sliding step with leading right foot
omote	left-side of the *shinai*
sage-tō	holding *shinai* at the left side of the body
seiza	kneeling position
sensei	instructor

shiai	match	*tsuba*	sword guard
shikake-waza	technique to initiate a strike	*tsubazeriai*	close-contact fencing with the *shinai* is crossed in a vertical position
shinai	bamboo sword		
shizentai	natural standing position	*tsugi-ashi*	short step
shōmen	center *men*	*tsuka*	hilt
sonkyo	knee-bend squat	*tsuka-gashira*	top of the hilt
suburi	*shinai* swinging practice	*tsuki-dare*	throat protector
suki	opening for attack; unguarded points	*tsuru*	center cord of the shinai
		uchi	strike
suriage-waza	rising-slide deflection technique	*uchiotoshi-waza*	technique in which you strike your opponent's *shinai* in his attack and counterattack immediately
suri-ashi	sliding step		
sutemi	self-denial; acting without being too self-conscious		
		ura	right side of the *shinai*
tachi	long sword	*waza*	techniques
taiatari	body check	*waki-gamae*	guard position with the *shinai* at one's side to conceal the arm
taitō	holding *shinai* at waist level		
tare	waist protector	*zanshin*	positive follow-through of strike; mental and physical alertness against an opponent's attack
tenouchi	balanced strength of hands at the moment of strike or thrust		
tenugui	traditional hand towel		